LITERARY MODERNISM
AND THE
TRANSFORMATION OF WORK

LITERARY MODERNISM
AND THE
TRANSFORMATION OF WORK

James F. Knapp

Northwestern University Press
Evanston, IL

Northwestern University Press
Evanston, IL 60201

Printed in the United States of America

LIBRARY OF CONGRESS

Library of Congress Cataloging-in-Publication Data

Knapp, James F.
 Literary modernism and the transformation of work / James F.
Knapp.
    p. cm.
    Bibliography: p.
    Includes index.
    ISBN 0-8101-0817-8
    1. English literature—20th century—History and criticism.
2. Modernism (Literature) 3. Work in literature. 4. Management
science in literature. 5. American literature—20th century-
-History and criticism. I. Title.
PR478.M6K55 1988
820'.9'1—dc19   88-19732
                                                                CIP

Contents

ACKNOWLEDGMENTS

I would like to thank my colleagues in the English Department and in the Program for the Study of Culture at the University of Pittsburgh. Their continuing debate about what a program in critical and cultural studies ought to be has provided an ideal atmosphere in which to write a book about the interrelation between cultural change and literary innovation. In particular, I have benefitted from the intellectual generosity and the warm personal support of Paul A. Bové, Stephen Carr, Jean Ferguson Carr, Marcia Landy, Dana Polan, and Mariolina Salvatori. I am also indebted to Gerald Graff for the constructive stubbornness of his demand for logical rigor and historical specificity. And most of all, I owe a debt to my wife, Peggy Ann Knapp, for the model of dedicated, creative work which she has given me, year after year.

I am grateful for permission to quote from the following works of Ezra Pound and William Carlos Williams.

Reprinted by permission of New Directions Publishing Corporation and Faber and Faber, Ltd.: Ezra Pound, *Personae*, copyright 1926 by Ezra Pound. *The Cantos of Ezra Pound*, © 1934, 1937, 1940, 1948, 1956, 1962, 1963, 1966, 1968 by Ezra Pound; 1972 by the Estate of Ezra Pound.

Reprinted by permission of New Directions Publishing Corporation and Carcanet Press, Ltd.: William Carlos Williams, *Collected Poems, Volume I: 1909–1939*, copyright 1938 by New Directions Publishing Corporation. William Carlos Williams, *Collected Later Poems*, copyright 1944, 1948 by William Carlos Williams.

Reprinted by permission of New Directions Publishing Corporation and Penguin Books, Ltd.: William Carlos Williams, *Paterson*, copyright © 1946, 1948, 1949, 1951, 1958 by William Carlos Williams; 1963 by Florence Williams.

Parts of Chapter 2 first appeared in *boundary 2*, and I would like to thank William V. Spanos for permission to reprint them here.

Introduction

The Discourse of Scientific Management

———————————— **I** ————————————

In 1921, during the administration of Warren G. Harding, the American economy suffered a serious recession. My grandfather worked in the iron foundries of northern Indiana during those years. When the business slump took away his job, he set out on a bicycle and rode from Muncie, Indiana, through all the industrial districts of Chicago to Milwaukee looking for work. He found no work, but along the shores of Lake Michigan he did find a great many seashells, which he kept. Some years later he visited one of his children in New York, and there he collected more shells. Later still, he made a little wooden box to hold the shells, and he gave them to me. There are two labels pasted onto the lid of the box. The first one reads, "Small snail shells are from the shores of Lake Michigan. They have been lacquered to accent their lovely markings." And the second: "These large snail shells are from the shores of the great Atlantic Ocean." Although this is a book about modern art and modern work, these two texts lie at the heart of what it is I am setting out to understand.

There is a kind of innocence in these sentences, of course, an innocence from a time before mass media and cheap travel had made the world so much smaller, so familiar. But there is also a deeply felt aesthetic awareness, a sense of awe before the beauty of small details and the mysterious otherness of something which deserved a phrase no one would use now: "the shores of the great Atlantic Ocean." His

1

small project was rooted in a sense of wonder and a lifelong curiosity about the nature of things. Such feelings of wonder and curiosity certainly have not died out, as witness the heavy equipment operator who spoke to Studs Terkel about moving earth: "You tear somethin' up that you know has taken years and years and years . . . and you dig into rock. You get to talkin' about the glacier went through there and what caused this particular rock to come out of the bank like it does. You see things come out of that bank that haven't been moved for years. When you see 'em, you have to think about 'em."[1] And yet there is always something surprising about statements such as this. Most likely, our surprise is that of the college kid working summers in a steel mill (also reported by Terkel) who is shocked to see a *real* steelworker with a book in his hip pocket. His surprise has less to do with the realities of a world in which anyone might pick up a seashell, or imagine glaciers, or read a book, than it does with the conventional expectations of a society in which knowing and doing have come to be seen as different, even contradictory, activities.

There is nothing new about excluding subordinate classes from the possession of knowledge. The fierce opposition to Wycliffite attempts to give the fourteenth-century peasantry access to the vernacular Bible was at least as great as nineteenth-century anxieties about educating the children of the working class. However, the ideology of knowledge has altered steadily over the centuries. With the maturing industrial society of the early twentieth century, it began to shape experience in new ways. Science, art, philosophy all had become professional, institutionally sanctioned activities by the end of the nineteenth century, while building the "real" world was practical work, the proper task for men of decision or of sheer muscle. In society's dream of knowledge, the scientists were all mad, the poets hopeless visionaries, and the workers anxious only for the fulfillment of the body's work and play. The paradigm is a convincing one, and its interpretive power has seemed to be unquestionable even when turned to an object such as modern art. Literary criticism, for example, has often (though not always) taken the fundamental gesture of modernism to be a rejection of modernity's "tawdry cheapness" and a corresponding affirmation of aesthetic self-sufficiency. An unbridgeable gap is assumed to exist between the "mythic" works of high modernism and their historical context, characterized as a tasteless, greedy, and often violent materialism. Knowledge in iron foundries (and those who study it) seems incommensurable with knowledge in the avant-garde salons of Paris (and those who study that). Between these two poles of the myth of mind against body, whether that myth is reproduced by quantitative social scientists or by avant-garde artists, there would seem to be little space for my grandfather and his seashells. But his text exists, a kind of anachronism that might remind us of the English weavers of a hundred years earlier, who had carefully assembled and preserved their collections of butterflies.[2] His text is an anomaly, but because it is, it makes visible a pattern which has shaped the self-identity of everyone who lives and works in the world we are beginning to call "post-industrial."

II

This is a book about knowledge, history, and work. My aim is to undertake a sort of triangulation among three kinds of work, all of which are involved with the constitution of knowledge as a crucial site of social struggle in our century: the formal experiments of modernist literature, the institutionally sanctioned criticism of that literature, and the transformations in the nature of work which are generally associated with the term "scientific management." I am not setting out to write a literary history of the period, a survey undertaken to produce new readings of the "major" authors. Nor is this a social history of work, offered up in the traditional manner as "background" to the literature. Rather, I would trace the ways in which a socially dominant discourse of knowledge is reproduced—and challenged—through a series of texts that range from the marginal to the most fully canonized.

Even in modernism's beginnings, in the aestheticism of the young Ezra Pound and the "stylists" he so admired—W. H. Hudson and Ford Madox Hueffer (better known as Ford Madox Ford), for example—art is understood to be deeply involved with the work of factory, office, and scientific laboratory. As writers began to undertake more radical experiments in formal technique, however, a critical tradition came into being which had the effect of cutting off all notions that the work of art had anything to do with more mundane kinds of work. That critical tradition has played a crucial role in determining the social significance of modernist art. Although a writer like D. H. Lawrence obviously treats the world of advanced industrialization, the highly problematic nature of his involvement with contemporary history is often subsumed rather too quickly into the category of visionary priest. William Carlos Williams, on the other hand, is often admired for the homemade technical experiments which influenced a later generation of American writers, but given less credit as a serious critic of social change. The notion that formal experiment like that of Williams could be a powerful kind of social analysis, rather than a quasi-religious escape from the hopeless condition of modern history, is a possibility that literary critics have been much slower to admit than, for example, the poets of the Black Mountain school. No modern writer better illustrates the need for a continually renewed understanding that modernist literature is written and read within history than James Joyce, however. Most reverently canonized, most voluminously annotated, and, as exile from a backward province of the modern world, apparently most cut off from the concerns of history, Joyce nevertheless reveals an understanding of fundamental historical changes that were transforming lives wherever mature industrialization held sway. In each of these writers, the social shape of knowledge reveals itself as a mediation between men and women and the history they make.

Before turning to the literature of modernism, however, it is necessary to consider what the "second-stage," or advanced, industrialization of the turn of the century involved. The factory system of the earlier nineteenth century introduced major changes in the mechanical execution of work, and in doing so brought about enormous transformations in the lives of workers, most of whom came to the world of factory discipline from the very different experience of agricultural or domestically based craft work. Although the changes in the lives of working men and women were profound, they were largely incidental to the large-scale restructuring of the processes of production. By the end of the nineteenth century, however, it was widely believed that the advance of industry would not be able to continue at its past rate unless future improvements in the tools of work were accompanied by appropriate—and planned—changes in the workers themselves. Predictable uniformity was one of the changes most earnestly sought.

One way of beginning to understand the movement that was taking shape during those years is to look back from the perspective of nearly a century's experience. In 1972, a special task force on "work in America" made its report to Secretary of Health, Education and Welfare Elliot L. Richardson. In its discussion of worker dissatisfaction, the report indicates several generally agreed-upon "ingredients of alienation" and then draws a familiar conclusion: "As thus broken down, alienation is inherent in pyramidal, bureaucratic management patterns and in advanced, Taylorized technology, which divides and subdivides work into minute, monotonous elements."[3]

This report, commissioned by a conservative administration late in the twentieth century, serves only to underscore the persistence of issues such as worker alienation. Half a century earlier, Randolph Bourne had argued in the *Atlantic Monthly* that management techniques that turned workers into semimachines would lead to either rebellion or "inattention" of a pathological sort.[4] Earlier still, during the late nineteenth century, when industrial patterns such as specialized and intensely time-regulated work had begun to affect large numbers of men and women of the middle classes, there had been great public debate about "neurasthenia" and "mind cures" necessitated by the pressures of modern work.[5]

This persistent debate about the problems of alienation at the workplace must be understood as one kind of response to a profound and prolonged change in the nature of work. During the early years of the twentieth century, while modernism was beginning its attempt to revolutionize the arts, many kinds of work were undergoing equally great change under the authority of the movement known as scientific management. Gathering a number of tendencies which had begun to appear in industry for at least two decades, scientific management was hardly a coherent theory, nor did it meet with immediate acceptance, even among businessmen. Its fundamental assumptions, if not its pseudoscientific excesses, did prevail, however, with consequences reaching far beyond machine shop and factory. Frederick Winslow Taylor was the movement's principal spokesman, and the program he promoted so vigorously was really quite simple. It began by challenging the usual assumption of employers that competent workers must be found and hired. For Taylor, the "competent man" was not to be found but made, deliberately and systematically, by management: "What we are all looking for, however, is the ready-made, competent man; the man whom some one else has trained. It is only when we fully realize that our duty, as well as our opportunity, lies in systematically cooperating to train and to make this competent man, instead of in hunting for a man whom someone else has trained, that we shall be on the road to national efficiency."[6]

Central to this project of creating the proper kind of men is the need for central management to appropriate the traditional knowledge which has always been possessed by the workers, thereby initiating a crucial division between knowledge (defined as the proper concern of management and its new servant, science), and practice, the machine-like execution by the workers of plans laid down by others. The new system's demand for a division of human beings into types appropriate to the various stages of the productive process is far more radical in its implications than the familiar notion of "division of labor"—specialized tasks performed by individuals who are not fundamentally different from one another. The notion that good work and high productivity are the result of hiring skilled and dependable workers was simply abandoned: "In the past man has been first; in the future the system must be first."[7]

Notions of human subjectivity came increasingly to be regarded as sites of uncertainty and conflict, by those setting out to formulate a "modernist" program for the arts, as well as by proponents of the new scientific management. Like so many of his contemporaries, Taylor had come to see human nature as relatively open, receiving its shape within historical process rather than as the result of inborn character or constitution. In a 1923 article on "The Progressive Relation between Efficiency and Consent" in the *Bulletin of the Taylor Society,* for example, Robert G. Valentine argues against "the idea of life as a fairly static thing": "This error is clearest seen in the common statement that certain types of people, certain whole groups of people as well as certain individuals, 'are not worth any more.' The reason they are not worth any more is largely because no adequate educational process has been tried. The theory is disproved by our immigrants when they are given the right chance. It is disproved in the tremendous progress the children in our schools make over the status of their parents. It is disproved above all by the absurd implication that human beings are less the field of the inventive organizer than machinery."[8]

Though firmly within the progressive discourse of opportunity for all, Valentine's argument betrays its ideological basis when the parallelism of its three examples breaks down: real children and real immigrants are set beside a logical category (an "absurd implication") in order to combat the public's assumed hostility toward inventive organizers who make no distinction between human beings and machinery. The scientific reshaping of human beings is central to the program of Taylorism, however, a point that is made with great enthusiasm by Morris Llewellyn Cooke (an associate of Taylor's, and a mechanical engineer by profession) in his foreword to the 1924 volume in which Valentine's article was collected: "The progress recorded in the following pages is marked to the point of being revolutionary. It is only because we are too near to it that we do not recognize the fundamental character of the changes that have overtaken industry as to machines and process—and even more markedly as to men" (ix). A striking feature of this revolutionary remaking, however, is that there is little place in it for *self*-creation. Men and women are to be "made" only in a limited and functional sense in order to suit the needs of a system of production. And, moreover, that limited making is to be governed by a strict division of labor in which the specifications for the newly "competent man" are determined, without his participation, by a special class of management engineers.

The successful product of Taylor's program for creating good workers presumably would be happy to relinquish a degree of individuality in order to become part of an interdependent system of men and women all cooperating to gain higher wages by achieving the higher productivity which only modern, scientific methods could enable. At the level of practice, Taylor's system meant analyzing each task with precise scientific accuracy to determine how it could be performed most efficiently. Through experiment, for example, the optimum speed at which specific kinds of steel should be machined could be discovered. Or the motions of a human operator could be broken down, analyzed, and a particular sequence of actions prescribed. Simple physical efficiency was only part of the goal of this sort of project, however. Taylor spent a good deal of time on the issue of "soldiering"— his term for the practice of working at a deliberately slow pace. As long as the worker was in possession of more knowledge than his employer about how to perform a specific task, he could easily resist the employer's efforts to make him work harder. The issue was ultimately one of control: "To work according to scientific laws, the management must take over and perform much of the work which is now left to the men; almost every act of the workman should be preceded by one or more preparatory acts of the management which enable him to do his work better and quicker than he otherwise could."[9]

The key to this process, of course, lies in just what part of the men's work is to be taken over by management. What the managers are to do is "assume . . . the burden of gathering together all of the traditional knowledge which in the past has been possessed by the workmen and then of classifying, tabulating, and reducing this knowledge to rules, laws, and formulae which are immensely helpful to the workmen in doing their daily work." Taylor makes an absolute division of mental and physical tasks, appropriating all functions of knowledge to management, while assigning to the workers a purely physical role: "Thus all of the planning which under the old system was done by the workman, as a result of his personal experience, must of necessity under the new system be done by the management in accordance with the laws of the science; because even if the workman was well suited to the development and use of scientific data, it would be physically impossible for him to work at his machine and at a desk at the same time. It is also clear that in most cases one type of man is needed to plan ahead and an entirely different type to execute the work."[10]

Knowing and making could hardly be more separate than they were in this vision of two kinds of men so differentiated in their functions that they almost seem to belong to distinct species. By appropriating all knowledge to itself, Taylorized management deprived the worker of a critical tool in his struggle to retain some measure of control over his own work. As a consequence, many kinds of work were degraded into the performance of mindless mechanical function. And the men and women subjected to this process were to experience a still deeper loss by having their humanity subtly redefined as purely physical, excluding them from the exercise of mind. This latter consequence was explicitly denounced by workers at the time. For example, the machinists of the New England Bolt Company, in a 1913 labor publication, described the use of photography to rationalize the work process:

"Cameras to the front of them. Cameras to the rear of them. Cameras to the right of them. Cameras to the left of them." Pictures taken of every move so as to eliminate "false moves" and drive the worker into a stride that would be as mechanical as the machine he tends. If the "Taylorisers" only had an apparatus that could tell what the mind of the worker was thinking, they would probably develop a greater "efficiency" by making them "cut out" all thoughts of their being men.[11]

Imagination itself had become the specialized work of a limited class, rather than a natural part of everyone's life.

If the redefinition of the human subject was of crucial interest to members of the artistic avant-garde as well as to those working at the cutting edge of industrial theory, scientific management's fundamental rationale was equally significant for both groups. To the question of why workers should consent to be reshaped along the lines drawn by a new class of expert managers, Cooke offered a straightforward answer: "Law—essential law—must eventually become recognized in this admittedly complex area where individual and group human interests are in constant conflict—or rather constant maladjustment. Men and women as agencies of industry are, indeed, far removed from the category of machines and yet both men and machines in their conduct are controlled by law—recognized or not as the case may be."[12] The notion that the reorganization of work advocated by Taylor and his associates was unavoidable in light of natural laws, which might be ignored for a time but could not be evaded in the long run, was a powerful one.

Even more significant, however, was the tendency on the part of these writers to link their scientific determinism to a view of history as equally closed and inevitable. Henri Le Chatelier, for example, writing a preface to the French edition of Taylor's *Principles of Scientific Management*, argues that the public must accord to economic law the same kind of assent it has already granted to the laws of physics: "People do not as yet suspect the existence of determinate relations between different economic facts; that is to say, the existence of what we call natural laws. In the moral and the economic world, these laws are complex and difficult to study. They depend upon a greater number of single factors than in the material world; yet, like them, they cannot be evaded. In both cases the efforts which have been made to transgress these laws have ignominiously failed."[13] Chatelier then turns to an account of the failure of various economic experiments begun during the French Revolution, and from there to a still broader explanation of the progress of "civilized countries" according to the dictates of "absolute law." His conclusion portrays history as leading inevitably to the present system of industrial organization:[14]

> One of the characteristics of civilized races is, as we have already said, the disappearance of the small proprietor living alone on his land, and producing all that he needs to live. Specialization and cooperation have increased the productive power of man enormously; the great factories, with their many workmen, their engineers, their selling agents, and their moneyed stockholders, have made it possible to reach a production per capita out of all proportion greater than the results obtained in the past by individual workers. It is impossible to recede from this new type of organization.

When he goes on to discuss the implementation of Taylorist reforms as a way of solving the problem of how profits should be shared between employer and employee, Chatelier has already established that such local and practical issues are the only ones legitimately to require our debate, because the larger framework—of natural law and historical determinism—has been taken to be a fundamental condition which no intelligent person would question.

Frederick Taylor did not succeed in transforming the working lives of everyone in the industrialized world singlehandedly and overnight. But he did articulate and publicize patterns of organization which were becoming dominant in the society of his time. These patterns soon reached far beyond the factory setting which was Taylor's chief concern. Let me quote again from the 1972 report, *Work in America*: "The office today, where work is segmented and authoritarian, is often a factory. For a growing number of jobs, there is little to distinguish them but the color of the worker's collar: computer keypunch operations and typing pools share much in common with the automobile assembly line."[15] If the intrusion of this factory-like segmentation of tasks into "white-collar" work seems to be a late development, and very far removed from the concerns of contemporary artistic and intellectual circles, it is not. The social tendencies for which Taylor was such a convenient spokesman were not simply attempts to increase the efficiency of manufacturing processes through the application of scientific method. Early on, they touched the office as well as the shop.[16]

The potential consequences far beyond the factory wall of these new patterns of organization can be seen in a fascinating report commissioned in 1910 by the Carnegie Foundation for the Advancement of Teaching. The report, written by Morris Llewellyn Cooke, was entitled *Academic and Industrial Efficiency*. This is what the report's preface says about the author and some of his basic assumptions:

> Mr. Cooke is one of a group of engineers who specialize in the organization and management of industrial establishments and the installation in them of improved methods based on a scientific study of the results desired and the processes involved. The value

of the report, therefore, lies not only in the care with which it has been made, but also in the standpoint from which the investigator has considered college work. That standpoint is the same which Mr. Cooke takes when he examines a manufacturing concern.[17]

If in recent decades universities have indeed come to be more closely related to the industrial world—in their dependence on government-funded research, their increasingly corporate structures of administration, and, most recently, in the practice of undertaking joint (and proprietary) research with specific companies—the notion of examining college and factory in the same terms was not a familiar one in 1910. The fundamental assumption behind this endeavor was that all work, whether physical, intellectual, or artistic, was amenable to "scientific" reorganization for the purpose of achieving roughly equivalent increases in productivity.

Just as scientific management would divide mental and physical work in factories, creating a hierarchy of power based on the possession of knowledge, so the mental work of universities was itself subject to a congruent segmentation. Cooke suggests that the "many and varied duties" of the professor be carefully analyzed so that a task hierarchy could be established. Much of the work could be downgraded and performed by low-level employees, while "important functions" would be retained by a smaller number of professors. He regards the typical professor's involvement with the whole process of his work as quaint and expendable, and argues instead for a role like that of the architect who (in his view) strives to pursue pure design while "strenuously" avoiding all the physical details of actual building. One experiment that seems to Cooke to promise greater academic productivity was being carried on by the physics department at the University of Toronto. There, in the main administrative office, were files containing standardized lecture notes for all department courses, "written in rather a uniform style and all on standard sized cards." Like the work cards which specified the procedures for each task in a Taylorized factory, these cards could assure the efficient and carefully controlled movement of ideas, although Cooke argues that the typical teacher would have to experience a change of attitude involving "his personal relation to his work" before his "full efficiency" could be realized. Perhaps the most significant statement in the volume, however, is a simple sentence from the preface in which liberal sentiment cloaks a metaphoric revelation that all workers (including those of this supposedly elite class) were in danger of being reduced to the status of mindless cog wheels: "The human side of administration consists in getting out of the men who compose the machinery the most devoted service and cooperation of which they are capable."[18]

III

Opposition to the accommodation of man to machine had existed, of course, since that possibility had first been raised by nineteenth-century industrialization. This is Ellen Gates Starr, writing about "Art and Labor" in 1895, in *Hull House Maps and Papers,* and speaking for the necessary unity of mind and hand: "As soon as a machine intervenes between the mind and its product, a hard, impassable barrier—a non-conductor of thought and emotion—is raised between the speaking and the listening mind. If a man is made a machine, if his part is merely that of reproducing, with mechanical exactness, the design of somebody else, the effect is the same. The more exact the reproduction, the less of the personality of the man who does the work is in the product, the more uninteresting will the product be."[19] Although her critique is firmly within a nineteenth-century tradition concerned with the moral and aesthetic consequences of machine production, Starr anticipates the twentieth century in certain ways. As techniques of management became more sophisticated and more central to continuing improvements in industrial efficiency, critiques focusing on the "external" exploitation of workers (e.g., long hours, dangerous working conditions, child labor) were forced to confront the subtler dangers of a more pervasive, inward redefinition of the very subjectivity of those workers. The figure of man being "made a machine" assumed a more radical significance.

The most far-reaching attempt to understand these new techniques of social control within the context of modern history has been that of Michel Foucault. He has argued that the economic take-off made possible by the accumulation of capital in the West was accompanied by a "political take-off" which had its roots in new "methods for administering the accumulation of men" and which issued in "a subtle, calculated technology of subjection."[20] Although not concerned with recent history, Foucault's account of the eighteenth century's meticulous, "scientific" regulation of the body, especially with regard to school and the military (e.g., handwriting, military drill) illuminates the earliest precedents for Taylor's scientific management and time study. These methods were complemented during the first decades of the twentieth century by other techniques such as industrial psychology, "human engineering," and bureaucratic control. In all of them, human beings were subtly accommodated to a system which shaped their lives in important ways.

In "bureaucratic control," for example, individual and class differences are gradually submerged into the generalized culture of a corporate "family," so that ultimately (as Richard Edwards argues) "workers owe not only a hard day's work to the corporation but also their demeanor and affections."[21] For Foucault, this would be a specific instance of a more general social process in which "subjects are gradually, progressively, really and materially constituted through a multiplicity of organisms, forces, energies, materials, desires, thoughts etc. We should try to grasp subjection in its material instance as a constitution of subjects."[22] In formulating his project of "genealogy," Foucault rejects the notion of "a subject which is either transcendental in relation to the field of events or runs in its empty sameness throughout the course of history."[23] Instead, he regards the constitution of subjects by the discursive practices of an era as central to the dissemination of power, which then becomes something quite different from the simply limiting power which a monarch exercises through the threat of violence. This new, disseminated power is in a sense possessed by all the members of a society, who, having internalized it, henceforth discipline themselves. Such power is thus productive as well as limiting. While that productivity is presumably in the service of society's dominant interests and ideas, it may nevertheless be appropriated to oppositional ends.

When, early in the century, opposition did arise to the social consequences of continuing industrial rationalization, the two principal sites of contention were those I have already described as central to the ideology of scientific management: first, an appeal to the authority of natural law and historical inevitability, and second, the attempt to "remake" working men and women through techniques of radical specialization, deskilling, and the withdrawal of knowledge into an exclusive sphere of "expertise." Writing in 1934, Lewis Mumford emphasized the interrelation of these two areas, arguing that the dominance of the machine had been sanctioned by something like a religion insofar as "the machine and the universe were identified, linked together as they were by the formulae of the mathematical and physical sciences."[24] Mumford's chief purpose, announced at the outset, however, is to destroy this essentially ideological sense that technology—in the form in which we experience it at present—is the unavoidable result of a law of the universe: "To understand the dominating role played by technics in modern civilization, one must explore in detail the preliminary period of ideological and social preparation." For Mumford, the philosophical premise of technological determinism must have been accompanied by some kind of human transformation: "Behind all the great material inventions of the last century and a half was not merely a long internal development of technics: there was also a change of mind. Before the new industrial processes could take hold on a great scale, a reorientation of wishes, habits, ideas, goals was necessary."[25]

More recently, David F. Noble, while pointing out a certain naive optimism in books such as *Technics and Civilization*, has kept Mumford's voice alive in his own critique of technology. Noble argues that "because of its very concreteness, people tend to confront technology as an irreducible brute fact, a given, a first cause, rather than as hardened history, frozen fragments of human and social endeavor. In short, the appearance here of automaticity and necessity, though plausible and thus ideologically compelling, is false, a product, ultimately, of our own naivete and ignorance. For the process of technological development is essentially social, and thus there is always a large measure of indeterminacy, of freedom, within it."[26] Like Noble's, my interest is in understanding how history may come to seem so hard and closed, how the perception of openness or "indeterminacy" in history may be frozen out, so to speak. By examining literary culture, however, I would not only indicate the significance these issues of industrial change ought to have for scholars outside the technological community. I would also show that, insofar as the contention which I have been describing is as much over the control of social discourse as it is over tools and assembly lines, literature and literary criticism may play a unique role. Noble argues that technological development should be seen as politics, and that when it is, "such awareness awakens us not only to the full range of technical possibilities and political potential but also to a broader and older notion of progress, in which a struggle for human fulfillment and social equality replaces a simple faith in technological deliverance, and in which people, with their confidence restored, resume their proper role as subject of the story called history."[27] Precisely this question, of how men and women came to be the objects rather than the subjects of history, has been a central and continuing concern of literature and literary theory throughout the twentieth century.

By the 1920s, Georg Lukács had already begun to place the transformation of the subject at the center of his critique of industrial capitalism. Discussing the rationalization of the work process, he emphasized the human fragmentation that is a consequence of highly specialized labor: "With the modern 'psychological' analysis of the work-process (in Taylorism) this rational mechanisation extends right into the worker's 'soul': even his psychological attributes are separated from his total personality and placed in opposition to it so as to facilitate their integration into specialised rational systems and their reduction to statistically viable concepts." Lukács saw that, far from being merely a feature of efficient organization, a "practical" matter of no larger consequence, the fragmentation demanded by modern production has profound significance for the workers themselves, whose very subjectivity is redefined: "this fragmentation of the object of production necessarily entails the fragmentation of its subject. In consequence of the rationalisation of the work-process the human qualities and idiosyncrasies of the worker appear increasingly as *mere sources of error* when contrasted with these abstract special laws functioning according to rational predictions. Neither objectively nor in his relation to his work does man appear as the authentic master of the process; on the contrary, he is a mechanical part incorporated into a mechanical system."[28] By installing mechanistic law *within* the worker's character, rather than imposing it on men and women who feel themselves to be unique, modern industry creates a self-enforcing system.

Elsewhere, Lukács ascribes this disintegration of the human subject, as it appears in the work of writers such as T. S. Eliot, to modernism's "assumption that the objective world is inherently inexplicable," an assumption which, for Lukács, epitomizes what he sees as the modernist evasion of history.[29] In my next chapter, I will argue that Taylorism's fragmentation of the human subject, and modernism's equally radical dislocations of literary form (both explicitly described by Lukács), might be brought together in ways which call into question the view that modernist writing tended to suppress historical reference and engagement. However, leaving out of account, for the moment, his position in the wars that have raged around twentieth-century literary movements, Lukács remains an important figure in the European intellectual dissent from all that Taylorism seemed to portend.

If the destructive fragmentation of the personality was one possible consequence of the modern transformation of the workplace, it is important to remember that others writing in the same European Marxist tradition could stress the liberating power of work. For Antonio Gramsci, work was the crucial term in the mediation between nature and culture, and its significance lies precisely in its power to break the illusion that natural law and historical inevitability have created a world we cannot change:[30]

> The discovery that the relations between the social and natural orders are mediated by work, by man's theoretical and practical activity, creates the first elements of an intuition of the world free from all magic and superstition. It provides a basis for the subsequent development of an historical, dialectical conception of the world, which understands movement and change, which appreciates the sum of effort and sacrifice which the present has cost the past and which the future is costing the present, and which conceives the contemporary world as a synthesis of the past, of all past generations, which projects itself into the future.

The continuity which links past, present, and future in this formulation is not an organic one. It depends rather on the human activity of continually reappropriating the past—of performing work, which is in fact to make history. It is in the recognition of this activity that men and women come to understand not only their own power to initiate change, but also the mystifications which had made them powerless so long as they viewed the world as given, as constituted by magic rather than by work. By "magic" Gramsci meant "a conception of the world mechanically imposed by the external environment," whether that imposition has its source in "the local priest" or "the little old woman who has inherited the lore of the witches." Or, we might add, following Mumford, an unquestioned belief in the "universal laws" which, we have been told, determine the shape of modern work. Work, for Gramsci, was a means for countering society's attempt to restrict human consciousness through the imposition of various forms of mythical thinking. He saw all work as including both "theoretical and practical activity." As the act which opens history to conscious human intervention, work is not merely an instrument to higher ends. Nor, as a concept, can it be used to fragment individuals along the lines of their supposed natures and so place them in discrete, hierarchical categories: "There is no human activity from which every form of intellectual participation can be excluded: *homo faber* cannot be separated from *homo sapiens*."[31] As this statement tacitly acknowledges, however, by the time Gramsci wrote these remarks, precisely such a human differentiation was well under way.

The changes that were occurring in the workplace during the early twentieth century should indicate some of the difficulties involved in Gramsci's notion that work can be a kind of borderline between the mystified consciousness which takes all the world as natural, as a given beyond human power to alter, and the contrary awareness which sees history as a human construct. For Gramsci, the proper understanding of work could be a way to liberation, an insight opening history to human intervention. But the powerful movement which I have described had as a central part of its program precisely the opposite effect. Scientific management acted to restrict the sense of most working men and women that history was in any way within their control by invoking the presumed inevitability of objective law.

The critical task in this further concentration of power in the hands of a new class of managers was the appropriation of knowledge, which would henceforth serve the "rational" ends of scientific efficiency and bureaucratic control. A necessary condition for this appropriation was the fragmentation of the human subject. In the future, men and women would be defined by their differentiation within a system of production, each individual fixed by a new version of the old hierarchy of mind and body: from artificial intelligence to the human robots of the assembly line. Not just an issue to be decided within factory walls, however, this development involved society's most general structures of knowledge and self-identity. And if Gramsci's conception of work bore less and less resemblance to the actual experience of most workers, its rhetorical power nevertheless continued to sustain a political stance that insisted on seeing history as the construction, through work, of men and women.

Modernist art has all too often seemed to be in willful retreat from any engagement with the kinds of social issues I have been describing. Formal opacity, the privacies of the coterie, reactionary "mythic" programs: these were the ways in which modern art has often turned its back on the mundane struggles of work and history. And yet writers like Ezra Pound, D. H. Lawrence, and even such "stylists" as Ford Madox Ford were well informed about such issues as the recently intensified rationalization of the workplace. In turning to the work of a number of these major modernist figures, I will examine those places in their writing where such issues are treated explicitly, though my aim is not simply to trace a number of work-related themes through the literature of modernism. Because the contest which I have described— between those who would institute far-reaching new patterns of work and those who would resist what they regard as a dehumanizing appropriation of technology—is in part a contest for the control of public discourse, I will explore in some detail modernism's engagement with the most basic assumptions on which management theorists such as Taylor attempted to persuade the business community and the public at large. Those assumptions include the scientific inevitability of specific social and technological changes; a conception of history as essentially closed to human intervention; an appropriation of knowledge to "useful" ends; and the rejection of older views of the individual as natural and whole (at least in potential) in favor of a conception of the socially constituted subject, shaped to the ends of profit by a new science of "human engineering." Though logical terms such as "ideas" and "assumptions" are appropriate here, "discourse" is the most useful way of discussing these formulations, since the ideas come to us embedded in linguistic and rhetorical patterns that are both typical and socially significant. The modernist texts I will discuss engage most significantly with Taylor's ideas on this discursive level, precisely because it is on this level that the scientific management movement would transform technical ideas into cultural mythology.

The relation between literary modernism and its society is most problematic, however, precisely on the level of discourse—where that which is "literary" must define itself over against another kind of language use, consisting in the pragmatic instrumentality of figures such as Frederick Taylor. The temptation to let industrial modernity's definition of language go unchallenged because it seemed inevitable in the "real" world, and to retreat instead into their own private realm of ahistorical aestheticism, was always present to the modernists. But while that kind of explicit retreat from history became less and less common after the turn of the century, many of the writers who did confront the social and economic developments of their age pose a far more difficult problem for critical interpretation.

While recent scholarship has made a valuable contribution to our understanding of the early modernist perception of science and technology, important elements of the social reality of the time remain relatively unexplored. For example, Cecilia Tichi, discussing Dos Passos's account of the widespread influence of Taylorism, has argued that "Taylor is important here because of the implications of his work. Begun in the factory and extending into the larger culture, it shows the explicit machine-based relation of efficiency to human perception and action. Taylorism hastened the American public into a gear-and-girder world which made Everyman, and Everywoman, an engineer scouting wasteful components of life and society. The Taylorist American was the designer of an efficient world. Ultimately Taylorist thought affected a significant body of early twentieth-century American writing."[32] As journalistic myth, Everyman may well have been an engineer, but in social reality, Everyman, and especially Everywoman, was far more likely to be a worker, and thus to be experiencing a loss rather than a gain in the power to design anything at all. Only if the experience of most working men and women is left out of account does "efficiency" seem to be a natural development, welcomed by a homogeneous "public."

Just as I want to argue that the early twentieth-century transformation of work must be seen from the point of view of those who experienced it as well as of those who designed it, I would emphasize the actively political character of that transformation. For example, while Tichi offers an accurate description of the middle-class periodical literature which glamorized engineering, she does not question that literature's basic assumption that inevitable and natural changes were simply being described: "The American middle-class man, like his son, learned that modern progress was the result of ingenuity and the development and application of machines and structures all over the world. The family parlor magazine rack held constant reminders that the old American agrarian world was transforming itself into one in which machines and structures took a proper place in the field, on the farm, and even in the forest."[33] But lessons are actively taught as well as passively learned. The workplace was not in fact transforming itself, but rather was being transformed by the vigorous efforts of management theorists like Frederick Taylor, who worked tirelessly to articulate and to teach the lesson that this father and son were receiving. To assume the priority of technological change, and then to examine possible artistic responses to it, is quite different from considering the idea of technological determinism as a powerful rhetorical counter, highly useful to those attempting to bring about social change.

The tendency of literary critics—even those dealing with modernism in its specific relation to science and technology—to ignore the politics of language and so to discuss, as pure intellectual history, material which might as easily be seen as highly contested social discourse, may be seen in a comment such as this one:[34]

> Taylor himself gave the name "scientific management" to his techniques for labor management, and Dewey similarly makes a connection between mechanical efficiency and the "modern scientific spirit." Both Dewey and Taylor fail to distinguish technical from substantive reason and they identify the institutions of a technological society with scientific thinking. A similar failure to distinguish scientific reason, technological management, and commercial products is found in many writers between 1900 and 1930.

For Taylor at least, the identification of science with management was not a failure to separate the two, but, on the contrary, a highly successful strategy of bringing the two together. Although a phrase such as "the institutions of technological society" suggests something quite fixed and solid, those institutions were in fact being profoundly reshaped. As David Montgomery has argued, "the historical role of the scientific-management movement was to explain, guide, and justify the changes in the hierarchy of human relations in the workplace that accompanied the turn-of-the-century transformation of American industry."[35] It would be difficult to imagine a more effective way of explaining and justifying those social changes than Taylor's appeal to the scientific inevitability of his proposals.

For many of the modernists, Taylorism and its related ideologies had preempted certain forms of knowledge (primarily, knowledge as defined solely by its power to do work). Even as they adopted a variety of explicitly oppositional stances, these artists, like their aestheticist predecessors, saw only very fitfully any possibility of reclaiming a practical and worldly knowledge for their own ends.[36] Too often the result was that modernist art achieved a social critique which is far more complex and insightful than we had generally understood, and yet that art ultimately became symptomatic of the very modernity it had opposed. While modernist literature spoke loudly against the degradation of all kinds of work, it nevertheless tacitly accepted contemporary assumptions about the instrumentality of reason, and so reproduced within itself a social discourse which would deny to art any authority to address social and economic issues. For anyone seeking to understand how art may be dialectically engaged with the specific social and historical conditions of its time, these contradictions of modernism pose questions of crucial importance.

Chapter 1

Work and the Stylists:
Pound, Ford, Hudson

I

In an essay about cities of the future, which he published in 1928, Ezra Pound attacked the power of modernity to change its human subjects: "Mr. Edison has been reported as turning loose on the perfect city of the future with such phrases as: 'nerves to toughen,' and: 'the loss of acute hearing will be a benefit rather than a handicap to the city dweller.' Either Mr. Edison is gaga or he was pullin' the reporter's leg. We will not sacrifice our ears in favour of idiotic noise, and we will not cut off our right feet so as to make more room in the bottoms of automobiles. We have five senses and we are not going to put out our eyes in favour of acetylene glare."[1] If the comic violence of this pronouncement is a characteristic device of Pound's polemical mode, it nevertheless defines an issue which had been of concern to Pound for many years and which lay at the heart of the modernist project of stylistic reform which he had championed. Whether physically lopping off ears and feet or not, the world of mature industrial capitalism did seem to threaten the integrity of the individual, and for Pound the question of how to resist that world was always a pressing one. Resistance did not begin with Pound, of course, but it did take an important new direction with him, as poetry in his hands became more than simply a vehicle that might treat social change as its "content." He saw the new order exerting its power in the very structures of language—the same language through which he had set

19

out to make his own way in the world—and he concluded that such power might be contested at the level of literary form itself.

For many of the writers of Pound's generation, the roots of a new literature seemed to lie in the nineties, and particularly in the aestheticism of that decade, standing as it did so clearly in opposition to the growing power of mass-produced art and middle-class taste. Throughout the nineteenth century there had been opposition to each new stage in the industrial revolution—whether early Romantic organicism or, in later years, the medievalism of the pre-Raphaelites, the craft nostalgia of William Morris, or the lush Catholic ritualism of Ernest Dowson. In most of these gestures, there was a kind of resistance through turning away, an attempt to counter industrial monotony by creating alternative models for social value and behavior. Although such models could only shape the lives of eccentric subgroups within society, that was often precisely what such groups intended. The "pure poetry" and "art for art's sake" of Pound's youth could have no meaning apart from the bourgeois realm which served as background to them, but they clothed themselves in a rhetoric of self-begotten beauty which seemed to reject all of recent history out of hand, thus sanctioning the later view of modernism as a tradition of asocial aestheticism. When modernism came to be defined by literary critics, terms such as these were often employed: "First, Modernist literature is distinguished by its formalism. It insists on the importance of structure and design—the esthetic autonomy and independent whatness of the work of art—almost to that degree summarized by the famous dictum that 'a poem should not mean but be.' "[2] But Pound the aesthete, who carried poetic experiment to unprecedented lengths, was also Pound the man who felt that eyes and limbs were threatened by the likes of Henry Ford and Thomas Edison.

As exemplary stylist of the modern movement, Pound had preached to all who would listen on two continents about the urgent need to renew poetry as craft, to purge away all the old Victorian slither and return to a reverence for language like that of medieval Provence or Tuscany. He was by no means alone in his work of renewal, but when we examine the work of those writers whose precise and elegant use of language served as model to him, the same coexistence (so uneasy to formalist eyes) of social concern with the preeminence of style is apparent. One of the men most responsible for helping Pound to see "the errors of contemporary style" was Ford Madox Ford. Ford's great importance for Pound and his contemporaries has been widely noted, and he has been called "probably the most profound literary influence" on Pound, and "in fact the key figure in modern English letters, the pivot on which the work of renovation moved."[3] The best-known example of Ford's practical influence on contemporary style is recorded in Pound's own anecdote about the occasion when Ford rolled on the floor in derision at the inadequacies of Pound's early verse. According to Pound, "that roll saved me at least two years, perhaps more. It sent me back to my own proper effort, namely, toward using the living tongue (with younger men after me), though none of us has found a more natural language than Ford did."[4]

For Ford, however, it was W. H. Hudson, the author of *Green Mansions* and many fine books about nature, who possessed the style most worth emulating: "For me, then, Mr. Hudson is the unapproached master of the English tongue."[5] And again (in a phrase Ford may have borrowed from Joseph Conrad), "We wanted to write, I suppose, as only Mr. Hudson writes—as simply as the grass grows."[6] Pound also admired Hudson's prose, and in fact he noted its similarity to Ford's work in a number of essays.[7] Though obviously different in many ways, these three writers all represent the aestheticist privileging of style, and yet their artistic seriousness is finally rooted in a deeper concern that writing is their work, and that in the age of mass production, all work is on the verge of unprecedented transformation. Stylistic experiment is thus a part of that transformation, even in this earliest phase of modernism, which tended to look back, nostalgically, to earlier models. Regarded in this light, the relatively ahistorical status which some critical practice has granted to the beginnings of modernist innovation must be seriously reexamined.

The view which holds that the arts of early modernism were defined by their radical rejection of the alien world of matter and money has been widely accepted by critics of left and right alike. But it is important to distinguish among a number of possible consequences of this position. For some critics, the aestheticist rejection of social engagement is not only described but affirmed, as critic and poet alike seek some transcendent artistic refuge from a violent and "meaningless" world. For others, the judgment that early modern art did indeed turn its back on history is accepted, but that artistic gesture is then itself historicized, and, most often, condemned as escapist or bourgeois. If the first is the response of certain kinds of archetypal or new criticism, the second is that of vulgar Marxism.

More productive than either of these extremes is a third tradition, of which Edmund Wilson might serve as an early exemplar. In *Axel's Castle*, his important book on the origins of the modernist movement, Wilson is quite unambiguous in asserting that writers like Yeats, Eliot, and Proust all turned away from the public concerns of their day: "The heroes of the Symbolists would rather drop out of the common life than have to struggle to make themselves a place in it—they forego their mistresses, preferring dreams." For Wilson, that kind of asocial art cannot be applauded: these writers "will no longer serve us as guides." Nevertheless, in his conclusion, Wilson sees these artists as simultaneously reflecting the age, retreating from it, and offering a hopeful (if vague) promise of liberation from its constraints: "And though we are aware in them of things that are dying—the whole belle-lettristic tradition of Renaissance culture perhaps, compelled to specialize more and more, more and more driven in on itself, as industrialism and democratic education have come to press it closer and closer—they none the less break down the walls of the present and wake us to the hope and exaltation of the untried, unsuspected possibilities of human thought and art."[8]

Among more recent critics, Raymond Williams has taken a similar position in holding that works of art may express the dominant culture which has produced them while at the same time inscribing "counter-hegemonic" possibilities. Beginning with the premise that "means of communication are themselves means of production," Williams argues that literary texts are a part of the general historical development of society, and bear a complex and variable relationship to that larger pattern of development: "These historical variations include both relative homologies between the means of communication and more general social productive forces and relationships, and, most marked in certain periods, contradictions of both general and particular kinds."[9] When modernist literature is seen in this way, as part of an interdependent whole rather than as a kind of soul trapped in the gross body of modern industrial society, then its existence as both homology and contradiction of that industrial society assumes important new meaning. A literary text may thus engage with a movement such as scientific management in three ways: it may take social and economic change as its explicit content; it may understand its own work as *analogous* to other kinds of work within society (e.g., the poet as "craftsman"); or, most fundamentally, it may render visible those general discursive patterns which in any given era have been appropriated to shape the possibilities of knowledge and of human interaction. Although I will consider examples of all three of these possibilities, my main emphasis will be on the last—that is, on that ground of social discourse where scientific management and modernist literature meet to contest the use of knowledge-as-power to shape social relations.

II

As a writer of exotic romances, natural history, and travel books, W. H. Hudson might well appeal to a young aesthete seeking to escape from the pressures of industrial change. And yet Pound saw more than that in Hudson's elegant style and nostalgic subject matter. He saw a social critique much like his own. In 1920 the *Little Review* published a special issue in honor of Hudson, and Pound contributed an article in which he related Hudson's vision to his own. Quoting passages in which Hudson deplores the callous indifference of men who drive one species after another to extinction, Pound points to the similar process which he sees as destroying the world's heritage of great art. He then offers an explanation:

> Yet if an anthropologist may speak out of his pages to the "naturalist," it is not only the bird and furred beast that suffer. A bloated usury, a cowardly and snivelling politics, a disgusting financial system, the sadistic curse of Christianity work together, not only that an hundred species of wild fowl and beast shall give way before the advance of industry, i.e., that the plains be covered with uniform and verminous sheep, bleating in perfect social monotony; but in our alleged "society" the same tendencies and the same urge that the bright plumed and the fine voiced species of the genus anthropos, the favoured of the gods, the only part of humanity worth saving, is attacked. The milkable human cows, the shearable human sheep are invited by the exploiters, and all other regarded as *caput lupinum*, dangerous.[10]

It is important to get beyond Pound's heightened rhetoric to see precisely what it is that he asserts in this characteristic passage. First of all, he assumes that the world of man and that of nature are one, that the destruction of plants and animals which Hudson decries is directly related to the social oppression which so rouses his own anger. The exploitation of nature is only one effect of a system of social order which is, in its essence, exploitative. Second, he asserts that it is the economic order of society which is determining. If there is a clear suggestion of his future obsession with usury and with Jewish conspiracy, at this point Pound is still concerned with other issues as well. In particular, he singles out one crucial aspect of the present economic order: the transformation of living beings into units which are as uniform and predictable as possible, and which have all been selected or altered in such a way as to maximize profits. Whether through monoculture and selective breeding in the sphere of nature, or through education in the human realm, the drive to create a world of profitable uniformity has for Pound a single effect: "And for the same system man is degraded, and the wild beasts destroyed."

In making assertions of these kinds, however, Pound is not simply using Hudson (the "naturalist" he addresses in the passage quoted above) as a convenient screen on which to project his own opinions. The work of Hudson's which Pound admired most, calling it "art of a very high order," was *A Shepherd's Life*, and Pound praises it with characteristic wit: "it should be some indication of Hudson's style that it has carried even me through a volume entitled *A Shepherd's Life*, a title which has no metaphorical bearing, but deals literally with the subject indicated."[11] The biography of a shepherd, Caleb Bawcombe, who had spent all his life in the downlands of southern England, the book's tone is often nostalgic, as it probes memories which reach far back into the nineteenth century. But Hudson frames his work with a clear sense of change, in the natural world as well as the human, change moving steadily forward under the pressure of social, technological, and economic development. Lured by the potential profits of rising grain prices, men had begun to bring the downs under cultivation, initiating general deterioration in an ecological system far better suited to the older grazing economy. As the land came to be seen more narrowly in terms of its capacity to produce cash, the peasants also suffered, losing their ancient rights to gather wood and pasture animals on the commons. For Hudson, the modern landowner's passion for pheasant hunting became a kind of touchstone for the insensitivity to man and nature alike of this new economy. Nurtured at the expense of all other wild game, which was consciously exterminated by the gamekeepers, the pheasant served to divide even further the peasants from the master.

One of the clearest instances of the painful process of "modernization" is Hudson's account, in A Shepherd's Life, of the agricultural riots of 1831, "when the introduction of labour-saving machinery in agriculture sent the poor farm-labourers mad all over England."[12] Strongly sympathetic toward "these poor labourers, poor, spiritless slaves as they had been made by long years of extremest poverty and systematic oppression," Hudson is quite explicit about the economic exploitation which was at the heart of these riots: "the oppression had made them mad; the introduction of thrashing machines was but the last straw, the culminating act of the hideous system followed by landlords and their tenants—the former to get the highest possible rent for his land, the other to get his labour at the lowest possible rate."[13]

This account reveals a significant ambivalence in Hudson's view of the problem of historical change. On the one hand, he presents very clearly the painful consequences of the kind of technological change which buys greater profits at the expense of the displaced working men and women, who must see their small wages reduced even further. By implication, Hudson would seem to affirm an older way, free of those modern kinds of exploitation which have been so devastating to the land and the people alike. And yet A Shepherd's Life presents a very striking picture of the evils of the past as well: the terrible justice which could send a poor man to the gallows for stealing half a crown, or the desperate poverty of winter, when the laborers were simply laid off until the farmers needed them again. Hudson is particularly harsh in condemning the old, feudal presence of a "great man" in a village: "I may have no personal objection to him—he is sometimes almost, if not quite, human; what I heartily dislike is the effect of his position (that of a giant among pigmies) on the lowly minds about him, and the servility, hypocrisy, and parasitism which spring up and flourish in his wide shadow whether he likes these moral weeds or not."[14]

Severely qualified as it is by a knowledge of the harsher realities of life in earlier days, Hudson's description of Caleb Bawcombe is still primarily a backward look, a celebration of the wholeness which a man like Caleb could know in his life and his work. Hudson ends his book with a remark that Caleb had made near the end of his life: "I don't say that I want to have my life again, because 'twould be sinful. We must take what is sent. But if 'twas offered to me and I was told to choose my work, I'd say, Give me my Wiltsheer Downs again and let me be a shepherd there all my life long."[15] The shepherd's work which Caleb would choose again is hard and lonely, it would seem, and yet Hudson has prepared this moment through the entire book. Chapter by chapter, Caleb's work is shown to be something whole, a task which demands physical strength and endurance, but also the knowledge and skill to train a dog, nurture sheep, to understand the land and the seasons. Free to learn more each year about nature's intricate process, and free to organize his own work in his own way, Caleb was not made to suppress a part of himself for the sake of earning a living.

The kind of wholeness which Hudson ascribes to the life of Caleb Bawcombe obviously shares something with that organic conception of society which grew up in the nineteenth century as a critique (from both conservative and socialistic thinkers) of the abuses of the prevailing economic system.[16] There is an important difference, however, between the nineteenth-century vision of organic unity and the assumptions under which Hudson proceeds—assumptions which clearly point toward the new century. In Hudson, there is little suggestion that the "organic" wholeness which he values simply "grows" when society is permitted to assume its "natural" shape. On the contrary, Hudson assumes that society is always made by human beings, through the structures of work which they create. This assumption is revealed with particular clarity in a distinction, made several times through the book, between Caleb and various gamekeepers. Unlike the shepherd, with his vast store of information and anecdote having to do with nature, the gamekeeper is a man who, even after a lifetime of work in the woods, remembers nothing of what he has seen there: "His business in the woods is to kill, and the reflex effect is to extinguish all interest in the living animal—in its life and mind. It would, indeed, be a wonderful thing if he could remember any singular action or appearance of an animal which he had witnessed before bringing his gun automatically to his shoulder."[17] Human nature has nothing to do with this distinction between Caleb and a gamekeeper who may well start out "with the liveliest interest in, even with sympathy for, the wild creatures amidst which he will spend his life." But while the one is permitted to grow in experience and imagination by the nature of his work, the other is made less than he was by a task which forces him to see the world through a narrow grid: protect the pheasants for the rich to hunt; kill everything else.

If Hudson's writing anticipates some of the assumptions that would characterize twentieth-century debates about work (e.g., the notion that subjectivity is not a stable essence, but may be shaped by the structure of work), his is finally a nineteenth-century vision. Work for Hudson is a kind of moral norm. In his essay on Hudson, however, Pound compares *A Shepherd's Life* to a similar book by Ford Madox Ford, *The Heart of the Country*. While Ford and Hudson are linked primarily because both are exemplary stylists in Pound's eyes, Ford's writing also looks to the future. In Pound's words, "Hueffer [Ford] is perhaps at his best when he approaches most closely to Hudson's subject matter; when he is least clever, when he is most sober in his recording of country life."[18] Published in 1906, four years earlier than *A Shepherd's Life, The Heart of the Country* does indeed share many of the qualities of Hudson's work. A fairly rambling account of Ford's observations of life in the English countryside, the book contains a similar ambivalence with regard to rural economy. Like Hudson, Ford is acutely aware of the brutally hard life of the farm laborer: "His diet is atrocious; it is atrociously cooked: his cottage, as a rule, is insanitary, draughty, damp, and too small. His work is too hard, his opportunities for mental relaxation pitifully too restricted. Except for his open air life—which caused a great deal of over-exposure—he has very little to keep him in either mental or bodily health. And I do not really see why he should want to live." Ford goes on, however, to conclude that this laborer is "the basis, the bedrock upon which the social fabric of our countrysides must rest. If there be a heart of the country, he is the heart of the heart."[19] This ideal of "the bedrock" has been taken by critics to be a kind of norm for Ford's characters as well as for his view of history.[20] But Ford knew that the old life of the country was rapidly passing out of existence, and if he recreates it with some nostalgia, he nevertheless refuses to allow his portraits to authorize any myth of a golden age.

When Pound writes that Ford had "wanted young England to see young England from London, from Sussex," he alludes to *The Soul of London*, an account of urban life to which *The Heart of the Country* was a sequel.[21] Ford's treatment of the city, which he saw attracting that generation of farm laborers who were steadily leaving the land, reveals considerable insight into the ways in which modern life was changing, not only for these recent arrivals but for men and women long part of the industrial world. In many ways, Ford was carrying on interests received from his grandfather, Ford Madox Brown, whose great painting, *Work*, had rendered a sympathetic portrait of the nineteenth-century industrial worker. In one particularly striking anecdote, Ford describes two workers. One is a railway signalman who works long hours at a tedious and exhausting job, and who then spends all his spare time and money constructing paper models of every cathedral in England. The other, a bus conductor, wants to ride his bicycle over every single road in England. For Ford, these obsessions are "simply mental anodynes" which are "necessary for self-preservation" in the face of work which is increasingly destructive of any kind of personal wholeness:

> In the minds of these workers work itself becomes an endless monotony; there is no call at all made upon the special craftsman's intellect which is in all the human race. It is a ceaseless strain upon the nerves and upon the muscles. It crushes out the individuality, and thus leisure time ceases to be a season of rest, of simple lying still and doing nothing. One needs, on the contrary, to assert one's individuality, and to still the cry of one's nerves. This leads to these hobbies which, psychologically considered, are a form of new work making some appeal to our special temperaments.[22]

In attacking the monotonous, dehumanizing routine of industrial labor, Ford was continuing a critical tradition begun in the early stages of the Industrial Revolution. Earlier critics, however, had focused on the moral wrongs of entrepreneurial capitalists who subjected their workers to hard and dangerous work, for low pay, in the worst of surroundings. For Ford, the crisis of work was not confined to the factory, but had spread throughout society, and it could no longer be traced to the greed of a small class of inhumane masters. The personal oppressions of an earlier era had begun to be imbedded in the very organization of work itself, initiating a crisis at once more general and more insidious.

Like many people in Edwardian England, Ford associated this crisis with Germany—or with what was coming in the press to be known as the "German threat." But Ford's knowledge of the threat was more specific than that offered by the popular press. He knew that in Germany profound changes in the nature of work were being explored, and he is explicit in referring to specific developments such as the appropriation of science to a new role as servant of industry, the institution of an educational system to provide properly trained workers, and the rationalized organization of the work itself.[23]

Ford, in his experiments with literary impressionism, captured this newly emerging aspect of life in descriptions like this one, of a construction crane viewed from a passing train:

> It was impressive enough—the modern spirit expressing itself in terms not of men but of forces, we gliding by, the timbers swinging up, without any visible human action in either motion. No doubt men were at work in the engine-belly of the crane, just as others were very far away among the dynamos that kept us moving. But they were

> sweating invisible. That, too, is the Modern Spirit: great organizations run by men as impersonal as the atoms of our own frames, noiseless, and to all appearances infallible.[24]

But Ford could also speak about the smaller details of an environment characterized more and more by this pervasive anonymity, this trivializing of human identity. He saw that the modern organization of work was shaping office as well as factory: "And in just the same way in offices, a partner mentions the drift of a letter to a clerk, he dictates it to a shorthand type-writer, she writes and addresses it, a boy posts it. And the clerk, the type-writer and the boy go on doing the same thing from the beginning of the working day to the end without interest and without thought."[25] Whether they make watches, or trousers, or (as we would have it now) "process information" in offices, the men and women Ford describes have lost the experience of seeing their work whole. Possessed of skills that are increasingly narrow and mechanical, they can only perform routine tasks within a much larger context which it is not their business to understand.

Like Hudson's gamekeeper and shepherd, the bureaucrats and secretaries described by Ford have all been shaped by the structures of work which they experience. Regarded in this light, even the simplest anecdote may suddenly reveal human experience to be radically historical. Hudson had posited no "natural" difference between his two men, offering us instead a gamekeeper whose power to perceive, to know, and to act had all been given shape by the constraints of his work in the service of affluent leisure. And Pound too was fascinated by the power of historical change to alter human "nature":

> The type of man who built railways, cleared the forest, planned irrigation, is different from the type of man who can hold on to the profits of subsequent industry. Whereas this first man was a man of dreams, in a time when dreams paid, a man of adventure, careless— this latter is a close person, acquisitive, rapacious, tenacious. The first man had personality, and was, "god damn you" himself, Silas P. Hacker, or such like. The present type is primarily a mask, his ideal is the nickel-plated cash register, and toward the virtues thereof he doth continual strive and tend.[26]

In making a comparison of this sort, Pound was not simply imagining that society preserves a reservoir of various but stable types, drawing on one and then another as need arose. He was well aware of the power of institutional structures to create the desired types, and wrote very clearly about this issue. Several years later, George Santayana made a similar observation that "a new type of American" would appear toward the end of the nineteenth century, driven by "the pressure of business enterprises."[27] When that new type did appear, he would affirm the common American belief "that whatever is is right," a belief which Santayana traces to "another sort of idealism, not at all critical, which might be called the higher superstition. This views the world as an oracle or charade, concealing a dramatic unity, or formula, or maxim, which all experience exists to illustrate."[28] It is this "higher superstition" which Taylor and his disciples had used in their efforts to justify scientific management as the inevitable expression of a history that was already closed—in the sense that it possessed a hidden unity or formula which need only be discovered.

Santayana continued his argument by examining the institutional basis for the production, through higher education, of the new American. He focuses on the reforms which Harvard undertook, beginning in the 1880s, concluding that by importing the model of German scholarship Harvard had begun to create a university based on the pursuit of specialized research, and that such a university "need have nothing to do with education, with the transmission of a particular moral and intellectual tradition":

> The teacher would not be a man with his hand on a lad's shoulder, his son or young brother; he would be an expert in some science, delivering lectures for public instruction, while perhaps privately carrying on investigations with the aid of a few disciples whom he would be training in his speciality. There would be no reason why either the professors or the auditors in such an institution should live together or should have much in common in religion, morals, or breeding, or should even speak the same language. On the contrary, if only each was competent in his way, the more miscellaneous their types the more perfect would these render their *universitas*. The public addressed, also, need not be restricted, any more than the public at a church or a theatre or a town library, by any requirements as to age, sex, race, or attainments. They would come on their own responsibility, to pursue what studies they chose, and so long as they found them profitable.[29]

"Profitable" is the key word here: at the heart of this new organization by specialization was an ideology of instrumental knowledge.

Like Ford and Santayana, Pound also knew that Germany had been in the forefront of the movement to organize work scientifically, and he argued that the German organization of intellectual work according to the same general model was dangerous. German scholarship during the 1880s and 1890s had inspired the professionalization of literary studies in the United States and later in England, and for Pound (who had experienced advanced literary study shaped by this movement) the consequences were destructive. Writing in 1917, he had argued that the German method was a way "of hammering the student into a piece of mechanism for the accretion of details, and of habituating men to consider themselves as bits of mechanism for one use or another: in contrast to considering first what use they are in being."[30] Acknowledging that dividing the labor of research into many specialized parts has a legitimate place in the advancement of knowledge, Pound argues that it is quite another matter when the worker is immersed in specialization without any possibility of understanding the larger project to which his routine task contributes, and without any genuine control over his work, since "in most cases the experiment has been merely blind experiment along a main line, in accord with a main idea dictated by someone else."[31] When work is organized in this way, a much wider human hierarchy must follow, with many more men and women dehumanized by their experience: "The student has become accustomed first to *receiving* his main ideas without question; then to being indifferent to them. In this state he has accepted the Deutschland über Alles idea, in this state he has accepted the idea that he is an ant, not a human being. He has become impotent, and quite pliable."

When Frederick Winslow Taylor published *The Principles of Scientific Management* in 1911, he was attempting to define and popularize precisely these recent developments which Pound attacked so vigorously. Taylor wrote that "in the past man has been first; in the future the system must be first."[32] Man still occupied an important place in his system, of course, but as we have seen, Taylor spent a good deal of time arguing that workers must no longer be simply *found*—they must be *made* in order to suit the new tasks which will be asked of them. Unwilling to let himself be hammered into "a piece of mechanism for the accretion of details," however, Pound not only took his stand against what he understood to be an increasingly general condition of modern work, he explicitly included literary production within that condition. Seeing his own poetic and critical "work" not as an escape from but as part of this general transformation of work, Pound set out to bend the form of poetry to his task of opposing this new and generalized kind of oppression.

III

It has been argued that "Taylorism presented new opportunities to writers in search of innovative form" and that

> Taylorist thought also offered writers a new position of authority vis-a-vis themselves and their materials. It redefined the artists' and writers' relation to their work in an age of assembly-line manufacturing from component parts. In the waning of the crafts era, it provided a new self-identification for the artist. One could now be a designer-engineer. For the intellectual center of Taylorism was not the worker, but the mastermind. It was not the rank and file but the engineer whose formulations would prevail and endure.[33]

It is not clear, however, that writers did necessarily identify with the engineers who benefited from the centralizing of power so crucial to

Taylorism, even if that centralizing was an "intellectual" one. In "Patria Mia," the 1913 essay in which he had initiated his discussion of the changing American type, Pound had surveyed what he saw as the sorry state of letters in America. Comparing the position of the writer to that of the industrial worker rather than manager, Pound identified the market-oriented world of magazine publishing as the heart of the problem. The terms of his analysis are particularly interesting, coming as they do only two years after the first appearance of Taylor's *Principles of Scientific Management:* "The whole matter is that the editor wants what fits the scheme of his number. As the factory owner wants one man to make screws and one man to make wheels and each man in his employ to do some one mechanical thing that he can do almost without the expenditure of thought, so the magazine producer wants one man to provide one element, let us say one sort of story and another articles on Italian cities and above all, nothing personal."[34]

What is noteworthy here is that in comparing factory owner and magazine "producer," Pound assumes that automobiles and essays are equally objects of production. He understands that "thought" is no longer to be a responsibility of those who perform the physical work of production. Pound, in effect, was applying industrial management to the apparently inappropriate field of writing. Scientific management did indeed turn its attention to the publishing industry. As important a spokesman as Morris Llewellyn Cooke could note with pride in 1924 that, at least with regard to the production department, "the book as an industrial product and each of its parts have been analyzed, so that the relationship of each part to the other and to the whole is capable of exact mathematical expression."[35] To be sure, Pound was concerned with the editorial process, and he makes it clear that he is not attacking the notion that specialists should write about what they know best.

The true object of his wrath was the practice of writing mechanically—without thought—to patterns already determined by those who manage the production of culture. It was writing of this sort which he would parody a few years later in his "Homage to Sextus Propertius." "Propertius" was an "imitation" of the Latin poet's verses (that is, a translation that felt free to take great liberties with the original). Like its classical model, Pound's poem set itself against the Virgilian epic, which had seemed to be all too ready to enshrine the imperial ideology of its day. Pound undercuts traditional epic diction by including words and phrases which remind us of the modern era of industrialization (e.g., "new-fangled" and "frigidaire patent"), and he mockingly announces that a new and better *Iliad* not only is "in the course of construction" but is being assembled "to Imperial order." "Rhetoric" was one of the terms which Pound applied to this kind of verse, built like a kitchen appliance to the latest market specifications and ultimately subjecting poet and reader alike to forms that served the power of others. British imperialism and the First World War were the poem's immediate targets. In setting out to oppose this threat to "de-skill" the poets by forcing them to assemble rhetorical forms already heavy with the culture's reigning ideology, Pound concluded that resistance would have to take place on the level of form itself.

In 1913 Pound had already begun to consider formal innovation as necessarily set in opposition to the constraining institutions of the literary establishment. Writing about editors who order books to standard measure, as if they were auto parts, he affirmed the need for open style, constantly changing to meet new conditions of expression: "Or, perhaps, I might express the situation more succinctly if I said: They are meticulous to find out if a thing conforms to a standard, like the carpenter who sawed off the books. But they have no interest whatever in ascertaining whether new things, living things, seeking for expression, have found for themselves new and fitting modes wherein to be expressed."[36] By 1920 Pound had gone far beyond this position, which echoed the nineteenth-century understanding of organic form appropriately shaping itself to varying content.

Hugh Selwyn Mauberley was a major gesture in the modernist attempt to resist the factory-like standardization of literature without falling back on older organic assumptions about literary form. As a poem about style, it has often seemed to express what many critics have taken to be the formalist bias of modernism: an aestheticism characterized by the highly conscious use of language, and by language as theme. Recently the argument has been made that Pound's earlier aestheticism had been redeemed by an awareness of the materiality of language, but that in *Mauberley* Pound retreated to an idealist and dogmatic kind of language usage which would henceforth govern his writing. Quoting Donald Davie's remark that "differences in tone of voice are precisely what matters far more than the identity of what is said," Paul Smith concludes that the poem's explicit turn toward social issues is a misguided one, that we are actually witnessing "literary discourse's retreat back into itself."[37]

However, regarded in light of the historical contention over the nature of work which I have described, a conflict well understood by Pound and his "stylist" peers, *Mauberley* may be seen as undertaking a project of formal renovation which insists on the "worldliness" of language—if that is what the opposite of an inward-turning literary discourse might be called. Taking as its subject the pressures of recent history which have led to the gradual deformation of the poet's work, and to the present need to strike out in new directions, *Mauberley* depicts the power of various kinds of socially imposed style to constrain human possibility. At the same time, the poem's own style, based on techniques of fragmentation and juxtaposition, constantly reminds the reader that actual utterances are always historical, that they bear within them the specificity of their speaker's place in the order of society.

The section dealing with "Mr. Nixon" is a good place to begin to understand Pound's perception that language itself is a crucial site on which men and women contend for social power. "Mr. Nixon" may well refer to Arnold Bennett, as Hugh Kenner first suggested, but he is more than a cautionary figure for the crass literary opportunist. He is also *words*, the language of a powerful discourse:

> "I never mentioned a man but with the view
> "Of selling my own works.
> "The tip's a good one, as for literature
> "It gives no man a sinecure.
>
> "And no one knows, at sight, a masterpiece.
> "And give up verse, my boy,
>
> "There's nothing in it."[38]

Mr. Nixon's rhetoric defines a particular kind of "realism" which assumes the production of salable commodities as its privileged norm and then uses that norm to shape the human beings who are placed in a position of subjection to it. Self-definition (in this instance, becoming a poet) is discouraged by an economic structure which quite literally starves it out, while terms of value ("masterpiece") are rendered meaningless insofar as they lack the instrumental sanction of the market. It is precisely this powerful discourse of advanced capitalism which requires that "Brennbaum" deny his own Jewishness. He must assume the uniform of banker or businessman and define himself by his "stiffness from spats to collar," rather than by the "heavy memories of Horeb, Sinai and the forty years," which must be suppressed because they would be personal, mythic, and without "value."

Pound writes that "the 'age demanded' chiefly a mould in plaster, / Made with no loss of time," but that demand is executed by men like the editors attacked in "Patria Mia," who hire writers to produce the goods, or by students emerging from the universities where they have been taught in the German manner "to consider themselves as bits of mechanism," or by men like Hudson's gamekeeper, for whom even nature has been made a factory to produce pheasants for the recreation industry. In this context, literature circulates within an economy driven by instrumental value, and Pound traces the entire range of that economy, from Mr. Nixon, as highly successful mass merchandiser, to the elite consumer of the literary equivalent of luxury goods, Lady Valentine:

> Poetry, her border of ideas,
> The edge, uncertain, but a means of blending
> With other strata

Where the lower and higher have ending;

A hook to catch the Lady Jane's attention,
A modulation toward the theatre,
Also, in the case of revolution,
A possible friend and comforter.

Mauberley could become a productive part of this system by simply accepting the discourse of instrumentality which governs this economy of producing and consuming, and which working class and leisure class alike have come to see as practical good sense.

He does not do so, of course—*Hugh Selwyn Mauberley* is about the rejection of Mr. Nixon's world. To be more precise, it is a poem which successfully rejects Mr. Nixon and his rhetoric of literary mass production and marketing by telling the story of a poet (Pound's alter ego) who tried and failed to reject that world. Resistance to the increasing power of the industrial age to force human diversity into the strait molds of productive efficiency had appeared in one late nineteenth-century form as the aestheticism of the nineties. That form of resistance was attractive in many ways to the young Pound, but in *Hugh Selwyn Mauberley* it appears to be a dead end. M. Verog, once a well-known figure among the aesthetes, now maunders among his pickled fetuses (as Librarian of the Royal College of Surgeons), dreaming of the past. His values are carried on by "the stylist," who has also retreated from the "contentions" of his age and now lives apart from "the world's welter," cultivating his garden. Both of these men are defined by a common discourse which had once set out to counter the instrumentality of Mr. Nixon's rhetoric through the aestheticist commitment to Beauty and the purity of art. Mauberley himself is given to us in their language:

—Given that is his "fundamental passion,"
This urge to convey the relation
Of eye-lid and cheek-bone
By verbal manifestation;

To present the series
Of curious heads in medallion—

In their isolation, their poverty, and their triviality these aesthetes simply confirm the hierarchy of value and social power which Mr. Nixon's words authorize—there is indeed "nothing in it" for those who defy the law of "common sense." Stylist and hack are thus bound together in a system which is at once mutually defining and mutually dependent. Both roles—that of operative in Mr. Nixon's word-shop, as well as that of powerless aesthete proving the wisdom of the market with every silly little poem—are constituted by a discourse which had begun to exert great new pressures on how men and women could imagine themselves at work.

At the end of the poem, Mauberley drifts away into a haze of his own South Seas fantasies. In doing so he reveals the utter passivity which has resulted from his acceptance of the aestheticist role:

> A pale gold, in the aforesaid pattern,
> The unexpected palms
> Destroying, certainly, the artist's urge,
> Left him delighted with the imaginary
> Audition of the phantasmal sea-surge

He is in fact no more passive than Mr. Nixon, however, and that is why he represents no viable alternative to the hegemonic society which has excluded him. Both technologue and aesthete are structured by that society, and though one is dominant and the other subordinate, each has surrendered the power of self-definition to an economic system which would remake its workers into instruments. If one is the figure for productive specialization, the other is its necessary ground: blank, proclaiming emptiness, confirming the dominant figure. As I noted earlier, we have all been in general agreement for some years now that this poem is about the gradual dissociation of "Pound" the poet from these men he might have been. Beginning as a stylist himself, Pound came to see aestheticism as the complement of the new Fleet Street crassness in the destruction of his proper work. On the other hand, only as a stylist could he counter this double threat to his vocation and his identity. *Hugh Selwyn Mauberley* depicts men and women constituted by powerful social codes, and in doing so it dissolves the invisibility on which such codes depend. The poem asks us to see the language which shapes us and to appropriate it for new ends.

There is what might be called a "meta-stylist" mode in this poem, a level at which style becomes aware of itself and attempts to become a critique of its own material conditions of possibility. The constituting rhetorics of a Mr. Nixon or a Lady Valentine engage each other in a process of mutual unmasking. It is at this level of formal manipulation, of disengagement from the power of any of the poem's "given" rhetorics, that the "Pound" whom we suppose to be freeing himself from "Mauberley" the aesthete is actually to be found. And it is this same level of formal innovation that marks *Hugh Selwyn Mauberley* as a significant expression of the emerging project of English modernist verse. As a poem that has begun to explore the radical potentialities of open form, *Mauberley* would seem to privilege language as the locus of modernist experiment. Yet this privileging of the word and of form is neither the hermetic religion of nineties aestheticism nor the asocial formalism which so much subsequent criticism has assumed it to be. Rather, it is the site of a struggle to reappropriate the power of self-definition through work, a power which Pound and his contemporaries saw being withdrawn from industrial workers, from secretaries in "modernized" offices, even from gamekeepers. And in the intensified pressure to write to fixed models for a commercial market, they saw it being withdrawn from them as well. For Pound, the narrowing constraint he would evade was manifest in the power of unexamined discourse to structure human beings into its necessary categories of hard-nosed businessman, or irrelevant aesthete, or social butterfly. In setting one voice against another within his "series of disconnected fragments," Pound was attempting to render those structuring languages visible to us as arbitrary and artificial rather than "natural" and thus invisible. By doing so he might place himself outside the power of those codes, mastering them instead by this self-reflexive act of language.

Chapter 2

Modernist Form and the Evasions of History

—————————————— **I** ——————————————

In much of the prose and poetry which he wrote before the *Cantos*, Ezra Pound engaged the world of advanced industrialization with surprising knowledge of its most recent innovations. With increasing sophistication, he used the form of his own writing as a means of resisting the pervasive rationalization of work by opposing two of its most important premises: that human beings should be remade along lines that would serve the ends of productive efficiency, and that this remaking was the logical consequence of historical progress, against which any resistance would be irrational and destructive. *Hugh Selwyn Mauberley* was not only the fullest expression of Pound's early opposition to the process of rationalization which had touched all parts of society, from warmaking to magazine writing, but it marked the end of his nineteenth-century style of opposition, an essentially artistic stance which had cultivated the aesthete's studied alienation. At the same time, *Mauberley* seemed to open another kind of opposition which confronted the discourse of scientific management on its own terms. The poem's experiment in techniques of formal fragmentation to depict contemporary pressures to constitute the human subject according to a discourse of instrumental reason resisted both the power of language to (seemingly) close history and its power to diminish the self understanding of all men and women. The *Cantos* promised the ultimate extension of this modernist assault on the appropriation of

37

language to serve the goals of economic power. In the end, however, they revealed only failure and confusion.

In asking the reader to confront the *Cantos* as an epic narrative in fragments, and to gather from its ruins a new pattern made out of unfamiliar names (Sigismundo, Metevsky) or familiar names made strange by Pound's new reading (Adams, Van Buren), Pound in the formal discontinuity of his poem implicitly supported its explicit rejection of historical closure:

> And even I can remember
> A day when the historians left blanks in their writings,
> I mean for things they didn't know,
> But that time seems to be passing.
> A day when the historians left blanks in their writings,
>
> But that time seems to be passing.[1]

The question which this passage leaves unanswered, of course, is whether history writing should always be characterized by openness and indeterminacy or whether there is in fact a single Truth which will some day be known, so that the blanks can be filled in once and for all. It is a crucial question given Pound's growing involvement with fascism, which sought to mythologize history, suppressing the reality of contending interests beneath a grand illusion of Destiny triumphant.

The discontinuous form of Pound's *Cantos* cannot be interpreted apart from the political developments which occurred in Europe in the decades following the First World War. But it is also impossible to discuss those formal innovations without examining the literary critical paradigms through which our reading has invariably been mediated. With regard to the arts of modernism, critical dispute has been particularly heated. From the outset, modernist formal experiment has been accompanied by apology, if not manifesto. The desire on the part of artists to "decompose" forms (Marcel Duchamp's word) was pushed to its limits by Dada, against a background of the Great War's slaughter. Brief though it was as a movement, Dada craziness mapped the uneasy relations of art and audience which continue to dominate critical discussion of the period. Tristan Tzara's defense of Dada poses the critical issue very succinctly: "We are often told that we are incoherent, but into the word people try to put an insult that it is rather hard for me to fathom. Everything is incoherent."[2]

Nevertheless, decades of formalist interpreters tried to redeem the "incoherence" of modernist works in a long, ingenious search to recover coherence by recomposing the broken forms into organic unities. On the other hand, socially oriented critics took Tzara's "everything" as their ground and sought the meaning of broken forms in the turmoil and change of a world outside the works. But in any case, discontinuity, whether manifest in the contradictory planes of Cubism, the montage of Eisenstein, or the ideogrammic poetics of Pound, has been an obvious feature of modernist art, and the more general notion that a breakdown in the continuity of systems was necessarily central to the modernist project has assumed a variety of forms. Paul Fussell, in *The Great War and Modern Memory*, has traced the pervasive irony of writing in the twenties to the human experience of a historical moment in which memories of romantic nature poetry, and conventionally beautiful sunrises, could frame a prospect of rotting corpses. From a quite different viewpoint, Marshall Berman has argued that modernism was essentially a way of adapting to a world in constant change, to the endless movement of destruction and rebuilding which is indispensable to the capitalist enterprise.[3]

For literary modernism, the statement which has seemed to cover all of these concerns about the discontinuities of style, audience, and society is T. S. Eliot's: "We can only say that it appears likely that poets in our civilization, as it exists at present, must be *difficult*. Our civilization comprehends great variety and complexity, and this variety and complexity, playing upon a refined sensibility, must produce various and complex results. The poet must become more and more comprehensive, more allusive, more indirect, in order to force, to dislocate if necessary, language into his meaning."[4] Eliot's statement authorizes the dislocation of language which has become a central mark of modernist verse, and in doing so it implies a critical practice which would have to seek out meaning as something concealed within a complex, indirect, allusive literary artifact. In this sense, Eliot's famous statement depicts a literature turning inward on itself, and so privileges the critical study of textual complexity at the expense of an examination of history or society.

But at the same time, even Eliot's privileging of language and form assumed that there was a logical connection between literary works and their social contexts: the necessary dislocations of poetic language not only mirror the present state of civilization but reflect the poet's urgent need to intervene, through a choice of significant form, in the apparent disorder of that civilization. Seemingly, Eliot's statement lends potential support to either side in a critical controversy which continues to the present day about the significance of modernism's formal innovations. At the extremes, the controversy pits those who condemn the modernist concern with fragmentation and private language as a reflection of the reified, bourgeois world, and therefore as an evasion *of* history, against those who celebrate the cult of style as a redemption *from* history.

In his 1945 essay "Spatial Form in Modern Literature," Joseph Frank offered what became a very influential formulation of the problem of the relation between history and the discontinuous form of modernist literature. Drawing on parallels with the visual arts, Frank argues that "depth, the projection of three-dimensional space, gives objects a time value because it places them in the real world in which events occur. Now time is the very condition of that flux and change from which, as we have seen, man wishes to escape when he is in a relation of disequilibrium with the cosmos."[5] Modern literature abandoned narrative representation for formal structures like those initiated by Pound's imagism, in which "a unification of disparate ideas and emotions into a complex presented spatially in an instant of time" must be apprehended whole, rather than read as a logically unfolding sequence. In this way it attempted to "remove all traces of time-value." Originating in the same perception of the modern world as disordered and chaotic which had so troubled Eliot, Frank's formulation sees the modernists as incorporating that cosmic disorder into their artistic structures. The very act of perceiving patterns of relation among fragments which seem to float in a unified space becomes an escape from time, an artifice of eternity. Discontinuities which in society are frightening become, when reenacted as art, the means to perceive a new order impervious to anything outside itself.

Although imagism is the purest prototype for this artificial recovering of order, the achievement of larger, "mythic" form is its true fulfillment. Following Allen Tate, Frank suggests that when past and present are juxtaposed in works such as *Ulysses* and the *Cantos*, "history becomes ahistorical." Thus modern literature is seen to be engaged in "the transformation of the historical imagination into myth—an imagination for which historical time does not exist, and which sees the actions and events of a particular time only as the bodying forth of eternal prototypes."[6] If this negation of historical consciousness is indeed an accurate description of the consequences of modernist form, then that form could offer little resistance to the ideology of scientific management. That ideology may be seen very clearly in a representative passage such as this one, from Henri Le Chatelier's preface to the French edition of Taylor's *Principles of Scientific Management*:

> The general diffusion of the belief in the existence of inevitable natural laws, that is, the belief in determinism, will constitute an enormous step in advance, even if these laws whose possible existence is admitted remain unfathomed. This belief in determinism leads one necessarily to consider in every case the possibility of attaining the desired end. On the other hand, in the absence of this belief, our efforts are squandered in vain endeavors to find the best means of accomplishing the desired end: federations of unions and of employers, political action, etc. Effort and money are spent lavishly, and society is overturned without accomplishing anything, whereas a few minutes of preliminary reflection would often have sufficed to turn one aside from an impracticable scheme.[7]

In this remarkably ingenuous statement, not simply determinism, but the belief in determinism, is the key to economic progress. Without that belief, society will be overturned and money and effort wasted in a "vain endeavor" to find the best solutions to social and economic problems. That is, we will continue to engage in such futile activities as "political action" under the mistaken notion that history is not already closed to our efforts. In this view, the power of political contention to change society is no more thinkable than is the existence of alternative technologies. The ideological implications of Le Chatelier's argument are strikingly similar to those of Joseph Frank, when he asserts that modernism's use of formal innovation accomplishes "the transformation of the historical imagination into myth."

Whether or not modernism does set out to disable our capacity to conceive of history as the product of human invention and struggle is a central question, and one around which much of the commentary on modernism has turned. If the form of modernist writing does accomplish the negation of historical consciousness, as Frank argues, and if this effect is analogous to scientific management's attempt to instill a belief in historical inevitability, then the question of whether Pound the artist was effectively opposing, or reinforcing, the program of Taylor the engineer hinges on how Pound's formal innovations are read. Among the critics who have addressed the contention that modernist form signifies an escape from history into an eternal realm of myth, Philip Rahv has offered what is still one of the strongest counter statements. Rahv does not dispute Frank's basic characterization about myth, agreeing that myth "promises above all to heal the wounds of time. For the one essential function of myth stressed by all writers is that in merging past and present it releases us from the flux of temporality. . . ." But Rahv then attempts to historicize the interest in myth among critics as well as writers, arguing that "the craze for myth is the fear of history" and that "one way certain intellectuals have found of coping with their fear is to deny historical time and induce in themselves through aesthetic and ideological means a sensation of mythic time. . . ." Rahv is finally less concerned with whether Pound, Eliot, and Joyce are truly "mythic" writers than with the fact that "in criticism the reaction against history is shown in the search for some sort of mythic model, so to speak, to which the literary work under scrutiny can be made to conform." It is this misguided critical practice which obscures what for Rahv is the crucial belief that "in so far as man can be said to be capable of self-determination, history is the sole sphere in which he can conceivably attain it."[8]

The sort of critical strategy which Rahv denounced in "The Myth and the Powerhouse" could take a number of forms. Cleanth Brooks, for example, regarded Eliot's method in *The Waste Land* as a "violent and radical, but thoroughly necessary" way of rehabilitating Christian

tradition which the poet was forced to adopt in light of the disintegra-
tions of his age.[9] Eliot's chief formal technique, the manipulation of
likeness and dissimilarity over a textual surface which has no apparent
coherence, was thus, for Brooks, essential to the construction of that
verbal artifact which rediscovers fundamental unity within its own
complex irony: "In this way the statement of beliefs emerges *through*
confusion and cynicism—not in spite of them."

In this new critical formulation, the poet as "maker" constitutes a
mythic truth which is alternative to the truth of science, and so stands,
as well, outside history.[10] On this latter point, Allen Tate is more
explicit. Discussing Pound's *Cantos*, he too emphasizes apparent
formal incoherence, the surface "jumble" and "puzzling contrasts" of
the poem: "His powerful juxtapositions of the ancient, the Renaissance, and the modern worlds reduce all three elements to an unhistorical miscellany, timeless and without origin, and no longer a force in
the lives of men. And that is the peculiarly modern quality of Mr.
Pound."[11] The matter of history is rendered essentially "unhistorical"
by its absorption into timeless pattern, and Tate sees that crucial
transformation as accomplished precisely by the formal discontinuities of Pound's verse. Yet Tate also sees that this rejection of history
has itself been brought about by historical modernity, though he
consistently refuses to take his own insight seriously.

The poetic strategy of creating an "unhistorical miscellany" is
possible in criticism as well, and the consequences are similar to those
which Tate ascribes to Pound's *Cantos*. In *The Counterfeiters*, Hugh
Kenner dealt more directly than other exponents of modernism with
the process of industrial rationalization and its relation to the discontinuities of modernist art. But while Kenner's would seem to be (like
mine) a historical inquiry, its effect is finally to render historical detail
so timeless as to be, as Tate put it, "no longer a force in the lives of
men." The historical details concerning the organization of work which
Kenner offers are set in a framework based on the rapid and surprising
juxtaposition of figures such as Andy Warhol and Charles Babbage
(who invented a nineteenth-century ancestor of the computer). Employing a critic's version of Pound's "subject rhyming," which he would
perfect in *The Pound Era*, Kenner places contemporary pop artists,
seventeenth-century philosophers, eighteenth-century factory owners,
modernist writers, and Victorian scientists side by side. The result is to
take away with one hand what has been given with the other. No
sooner does Kenner recognize the historical effect of technology than
he dehistoricizes it, effacing, for example, the enormous historical
differences between the first tentative experiments of the industrial
revolution, the full Victorian realization of heavy industry, and America's transformation into a "post-industrial information society." This
use of "spatial form" in literary criticism leaves little place for the kind

of historical specificity which, for example, would insist on the important difference between the nineteenth century's need to organize the physical processes of production and the newer emphasis (which Taylorism marks) on organizing human resources, through the invention of the concept of "management."

Certainly, the historical issues which Kenner examines are similar to those I have discussed. When he describes the first fully rationalized factory (a French silk mill in 1756), for example, he spells out the human consequences of mechanized silk making quite explicitly: "If a man does nothing with his life but spin threads, then just how is a thread-spinning machine not a purified man? And indeed it can replace him." Kenner's conclusions about the human consequences of an age of mechanism would seem to be very similar to mine, but in fact they obscure the sort of specific historical understanding which I am attempting to reach: "Much effort, in short, has been devoted to persuading us that we really are rather slipshod automata, which thanks to modern education can be taught a few things, such as Temperance, Industry, Exercise and Cleanliness."[12] This list of capitalized virtues is more characteristic of the mid-Victorian factory owner's efforts to indoctrinate workers unfamiliar with the rigors of industrial discipline than it is of the late twentieth century, to which Kenner's assertion actually refers. The historical vagueness in an observation such as this is not incidental, but rather part of a general interpretive strategy.

Like Georg Lukács (with whom he would otherwise be in little sympathy), Kenner regards the modern world as endlessly replicating the process of commodification. But while Lukács ascribes this process to the economic order of capitalism, Kenner looks to an epistemological origin in the modern dominance of "empiricism." And regardless of how closely related empiricism and capitalism may be, Kenner's decision to privilege a cognitive (rather than a political or economic) terminology is crucial: "Empiricism is a game. Its central rule forbids you to understand what you are talking about. The application of this rule, when we remember that we *are* playing a game, yields satire." It is within this larger framework of philosophical assumptions that Kenner then proceeds to examine what he calls the "countermeasures" of art and literature. He argues that writers like Defoe and Swift "counterfeited in a counterfeiting time," and that in our own century "the post-symbolist aesthetic" continued to reflect its counterfeiting culture in textual features such as its "suave surfaces, its unnerving discontinuities."[13] Although Kenner contends that these artistic techniques can "save us from debility amid the conventions of empiricism," they do not do so, in his formulation, by returning to us any sense that we may understand and change the stultifying world he has described. Rather, we are taught to distinguish that which is "genuine" from "the blandishments of the spurious," by learning to distinguish the voice of true genius from all those mechanical reproductions which mass culture purveys. Genius itself imitates those imitations, but only in order to remind us that its own meaning and value are independent of all temporal economic and social forces. Winning the "game" of empiricism thus means discriminating between the genuine article and the "tawdry cheapness" of the present world, but doing so by stepping out of the world of historical contention and change and into a realm of Art eternal.

II

The notion that modernist experiment issued in an unhistorical or timeless literature was by no means confined to the American critical tradition, however. Working out of a European tradition of Hegelian and later Marxist critique, Lukács had denounced the formalist bias of "bourgeois-modernist critics," with their "exaggerated concern with formal criteria, with questions of style and technique."[14] Like those critics, however, Lukács argued that a primary characteristic of modernist literature was its "negation of history."[15] For Lukács, the individual in modernist literature is solitary and asocial, reduced to a figure of the "universal *condition humaine*," and this transformation to the plane of the timeless is accomplished, significantly, through displacing the complexity of the world onto the complexity of the work itself: "The narrator, the examining subject, is in motion; the examined reality is static." While Lukács's bias against modernism has been criticized from a number of perspectives, his initial premise that such art purports to accomplish the "negation of history" goes largely unchallenged. Examining Lukács's judgments of modernist art in light of terms laid down in the early *Theory of the Novel*, for example, Fredric Jameson's observation is characteristic of the wide acceptance of Lukács's premise: "It was no accident that the first two chapters were so rich in suggestions and intimations of modernism: for modern or symbolic art is characterized precisely by its ahistorical, metaphysical way of viewing human life in the world."[16]

The central point of conjunction between the discourse of scientific management and the modernist text as read by this very broad range of critics (from Alan Tate to Fredric Jameson) is a shared assumption that for the modernists history is not indeterminate, open to human making. Lukács's argument is particularly illuminating with regard to this conjunction. He contends, in "The Ideology of Modernism," that modernism's obsession with psychopathology is rooted in "a desire to escape from the reality of capitalism": "But this implies the absolute primacy of the *terminus a quo*, the condition from which it is desired to escape. Any movement towards a *terminus ad quem* is condemned to impotence. As the ideology of most modernist writers asserts the unalterability of outward reality (even if this is reduced to a mere state of consciousness) human activity is, *a priori*, rendered impotent and robbed of meaning."[17]

Though critics of left and right, then, have been diametrically opposed over the meaning and value of modernist literature, they have nevertheless shared the view that modernism does assume the "unalterability of outward reality." Conservative critics have tended to believe that this contention is objectively true and that modernism's search for eternal truths of art or myth is thus a saving gesture. Marxist critics, on the other hand, have most often assumed that while the "unalterability of outward reality" is indeed the central assumption of modernist works, it is not true of the world beyond those texts, and therefore stands as justification for condemning the modernist project. Although my own sympathies lie with those critics, from Rahv and Lukács to Jameson, who would historicize modernism, I would challenge the notion that modernist form is ahistorical in essence.

More recently still, as post-structuralist theory has been brought to bear on modernist verse, the movement's presumed ahistoricism has continued to occupy an important place. Thus Joseph Riddel, in a curious echo of the humanistic criticism he calls into question, has argued that Eliot's poetry sets out to "heal the wounds of time." Riddel bases his analysis in Derrida's critique of the logocentrism of Western culture. For Riddel, Eliot's fragmented and allusive texts reveal a "nostalgia for the center," as they "reenact the gathering or regathering of the many into the One."[18] The very incompleteness of texts that continually supplement a tradition regarded by Eliot as at once complete and yet never complete, is itself the sign of an originating Word endlessly sought by a language which can only manifest the absence of that Word.

Although Pound's verse presents a surface that is equally fragmented and allusive as Eliot's, Riddel argues that imagism/vorticism initiated a kind of textuality which was not contained within a metaphysics of the logos. Rather than employing allusions which suggest some authorizing point of reference in the past, Pound is viewed as engaging in a process of repetition, each fragment of the past being reinscribed in such a way that Pound's new text neither replaces nor defers to the earlier texts it includes. Given a text which neither points to some lost, archaic center, nor exists in its own full presence (because continually alluding to the past), the reader of Pound's verse is confronted by the play of text making, "the construction of one house upon another." As a process of continual displacement and reinscription, Pound's verse resists all closure, whether that produced by the privileging of any one of its elements (e.g., authorial intention) or by a logocentric nostalgia like that of Eliot. This verse was based on a "superpositioning" of images, "the act of the second image displacing the first even as it carries forward the memory (trace?) of that sign displaced, negated, repeated, and effaced. There is no perception here, certainly not of nature; the natural image grows in a mythic garden, or text."[19]

In so delineating a mythic practice which is not the attempt to recover an archetypal center, Riddel departs from the dominant reading of the "mythical method" in modernist literature. If the deepest need served by that method, however, was to offer escape from the chaos of history into a timeless world, then this departure may be no change at all. As "neither exteriorizations of an interiority, nor representations," the images which constitute this verse "present only their own play of energies." Time exists in this play only as a medium for the expression of difference through the successive reinscription of images. A self-contained garden of myth, this linguistic self-deconstruction would seem to offer at least as sure a defense against the intrusions of history as any garden centered by the Tree of Life. So understood, this deconstructive distinction between Pound and Eliot remains within the formalist investigation of the ways in which linguistic discontinuity in modern literature "means." Like earlier versions of that investigation, it reads Eliot's juxtaposing of the discontinuities of modern civilization against those of poetic language as an invitation to explore only the latter. Social disruptions seem to be mastered by a myth of language which accomplishes Eliot's ends through the exact inversion of his terms: the still point becomes an icon of self-born, perpetual verbal motion.

III

In spite of its broad influence, the interpretation which holds that modernist form necessarily signifies a rejection of historical con-sciousness and an escape into myth is seldom questioned. I challenge this characterization of modernism and argue instead that its formal innovations may remind us that history is a human construct, and so serve to resist a powerful social discourse like that of scientific management, which depends on the perception of historical inevita-bility. In making this argument, however, I must offer two qualifica-tions. First, in saying "*may* remind us," I would emphasize that "modernism" is a very large and imprecise term which, for all its usefulness, refers to writers who are very different from each other, who often differed greatly from their own earlier "selves" over the years, and who wrote in historical contexts which changed enormously. Thus, Eliot's writings do largely fit the paradigm that modernist form enacts an evasion of history. Much of Pound's work, on the other hand, does not fit that paradigm, though when it does, it does so in a particularly destructive way. My second qualification concerns "form," which, like "modernism," is too often used as if it were something essential and unchanging, which it is not. "Modernist form" is an extremely useful term, but it too has little meaning when divorced from its historical specificity.

The notion that formal discontinuities of one kind or another can result in an altered perception on the part of the reader has been one important assertion about the significance of "modernist form." From Dada's found objects to Brecht's theory of the *Verfremdungseffekt* to more recent formulations, such as the assertion that Synge's plays created "cognitive dissonance" for their original Irish audiences,[20] much modern art has been seen as disrupting habitual patterns of perception in the reader or audience—generally as a program, though occasionally by accident. The serious difficulty with all such programs of defamiliarization has been pointed out by Gerald Graff in a series of questions: "But how can open, multiple forms 'lay bare' contradictions when they are, so often, themselves expressions of a viewpoint distorted by alienation? Where does literature get the perspective that permits it to present distortion *as* distortion? How does it make itself a criticism of ideological contradictions rather than a symptom of them?" Graff goes on to suggest that the effect of such techniques of estrangement might be "to confuse or disarm critical intelligence rather than to focus it," and that possibility is certainly a real one, particularly if we assume that literary forms themselves are intrinsically meaningful, independent of the specific historical contexts in which they are employed.[21]

Literature is always produced within history, however, and when we speak of modernist works as self-reflexive, we ought to question the familiar assumption that their reflexivity must be directed solely to formal issues of language and style. What the work is "about" may well inform the significance of its style, and vice versa. Edward Said has described what he calls "worldly" texts, texts that are themselves events in some sense, and which participate in "the social world, human life, and of course the historical moments in which they are located and interpreted."[22] In my view, it is only through the dialectical interplay of form and content within the text that any given form becomes meaningful—whether to assume the worldliness of which Said speaks, or to refuse any engagement with social issues, in the gesture of aestheticism, for example. No purely formal feature of a text (discontinuous fragmentation, for instance) can be interpreted a priori to signify either social criticism or acquiesence. Certainly, the lived experience of men and women in the Taylorized office or factory cannot be divorced from the textual authorization of that experience, in the distinctive discourse of papers and speeches like those I have quoted. And thus when modernist writers speak about similar attempts to foreclose history through such textual means (as when Pound, for example, represents "Mr. Nixon's" pragmatic discourse of instrumental reason as fairly bludgeoning its listeners into abandoning all thought of changing the status quo), then the writer's own use of a very different kind of discourse—open, indeterminate, and inviting the reader's active participation, for example—assumes a meaning it could not have had if the writer had not introduced the idea that language which presents itself as seamless and inevitable can be a means of social repression.

IV

Even to begin to understand the complex interplay of formal innovation and social content within the *Cantos* would require the rest of this book. My aim is more modest. I would suggest that Pound's long poem ultimately failed to distinguish between the symptomatic and the socially critical potentiality of modernism. The *Cantos* foundered on their own contradictions, contradictions which were as much a matter of historical analysis as of poetic strategy. As a generalization about Pound the aesthete turned Fascist, this assertion is hardly controversial, but the details are more perplexing. In 1917, Pound denounced the German model for organizing work because it led to "hammering the student into a piece of mechanism for the accretion of details, and of habituating men to consider themselves as bits of mechanism for one use or another."[23] He went on to associate this human pattern with contemporary attitudes toward machines themselves: "The bulk of scholarship has gone under completely; the fascinations of technical and mechanical education have been extremely seductive (I mean definitely the study of machines, the association with engines of all sorts, the inebriety of mechanical efficiency, in all the excitement of its very rapid evolution)." And yet two years earlier he had written in praise of Edward Wadsworth, the painter, by referring to Wadsworth's "feeling for ports and machines":

> I consider this one of the age-tendencies, springing up naturally in many places and coming into the arts quite naturally and spontane-

ously in England, in America, and in Italy. We all know the small boy's delight in machines. It is a natural delight in a beauty that had not been pointed out by professional aesthetes. I remember young men with no care for aesthetics who certainly would not know what the devil this article was about, I remember them examining machinery catalogues, to my intense bewilderment, commenting on machines that certainly they would never own and that could never by any flight of fancy be of the least use to them. This enjoyment of machinery is just as natural and just as significant a phase of this age as was the Renaissance 'enjoyment of nature for its own sake,' and not merely as an illustration of dogmatic ideas.[24]

Ten years later, in 1925, Pound was still interested in the aesthetic possibilities of the machine, as indicated by an excited series of letters to his father, requesting photographs of "machinery and spare parts."[25] Attitudes toward machines or technology per se cannot be equated with attitudes toward the organization of work, nor in particular the human consequences of a movement such as scientific management. But the ambivalence which Pound had always displayed in his attitude toward the mechanistic did make possible an increasing ambiguity, after 1920, in his approach to the technological transformation of society.

In the letters to his father, Pound expresses fascination with the aesthetic possibilities of the machine ("The NOSE of the big dies, for example, excellent shape. Photos of detail of the coin press, especially at point where the force is concentrated"). But he repudiates a pure aestheticism in a way which recalls the Vorticism of the previous decade: "In any case the regard to appearance is merely dillentantism [sic]. The beauty comes from the efficiency at one point (vortex)." Vorticism had shown great interest in the machine, partly in reaction to the technological boosterism of its rival movement, Futurism. The Vorticist depiction of technology tended to be far more critical than that of the Futurists, whether in Wyndham Lewis's drawings of the mechanization of the First World War, or in a painting such as David Bomberg's *In the Hold*, which Reed Dasenbrock has characterized as focusing on "the work process itself and the depersonalization involved in the system he is portraying." That the machine was contested terrain for these artists is suggested by Dasenbrock's interpretation of Jacob Epstein's alteration of his "Rock Drill," the most famous Vorticist work: "But Epstein must have thought that this version celebrated the machine too much because he later cut off the stilts, got rid of the drill, and cast only the torso to produce the work known today as *Torso in Metal from the 'Rock Drill,'* a study of mechanized man as a sinister but mutilated figure."[26]

In spite of the Vorticist critique of mechanization, it was at the same Vorticist period (1915) that Pound had written of the "small boy's delight in machines," and that delight was certainly to be found amidst all the Vorticist bombast. The machine could always be viewed as possessing a liberatory potential, even by those who denounced its actual uses, and Pound knew well enough that technology was not a given, that it always embodies human purposes: "Let me put it another way, they [machines] don't confront man like the *faits accomplis* of nature; these latter he has to attack *ab exteriore*, by his observation, he can't construct 'em; he has to examine them. Machines are already an expression of his own desire for power and precision; one man can learn from them what some other man has put into them, just as he can learn from other artistic manifestations."[27] This assertion (from the early 1920s) that the machine is an extension of human purpose offers an important clue to why Pound would soon begin to rethink the relation between his art and the complex social and economic developments of the times. The 1920s and thirties were decades of strange and shifting alliances, a point made very clearly by two international successes which scientific management achieved during this period.

Edward Eyre Hunt was a respectable member of the Republican establishment (as assistant to Secretary of Commerce Herbert Hoover) when, in 1924, he edited a book entitled *Scientific Management since Taylor: A Collection of Authoritative Papers.* In his introduction he recounts with great pride the triumph of scientific management which the First World War had occasioned: "Mass production on an immense scale, the need for greater and constantly greater output—these made of the principles which Taylor had laid down the highway to victory. . . ."[28] And among its overseas successes, he points to the fact that "even in Bolshevik Russia, in April, 1918, Premier Nikolai Lenin declared, 'We must introduce . . . the study and teaching of the new Taylor System and its systematic trial and adaptation.' " Complementing this triumph on the left, however, and touching the career of Ezra Pound much more closely, is the fact that the other notable international success of the scientific management movement during the 1920s was the official connection which it developed with the Italian Fascist state.[29]

Ironically, as he retreated ever deeper into the dogmatisms of his Fascist commitments, the poet who had begun by defying Edison's mechanistic vision of the future city found himself allied with the very movement which had brought the instrumental reason of modernity to its most concrete application. The scientific management movement was itself no more Fascist than it was Bolshevik. But if it did lend itself very easily to the new commitment within the Soviet Union to the centralized appropriation of technology and heavy industry, it also contained elements of a "populist" rhetoric which was mirrored by a similar strain in Italian Fascist discourse, and which could easily be appropriated by Pound as he fashioned his own peculiar vision of fascism as a reforming movement. The Italian Fascist variety of "populism" sought to downplay class conflict, "elevating instead the idea of 'the people.' Past history thus served to create a sense of destiny, of common purpose, aimed toward the future and producing the 'new man' whose life was consecrated to the service of the harmonious community and reborn in a struggle for national glory." The populist rhetoric further sought to "merge working class and petty bourgeoisie in the common goals of hard work, increased productivity, the subordination of private and class interest to the public interest, submission to authority and loyalty to the nation."[30]

Taylor's scheme for creating a new industrial man had none of the messianic aura of Italian fascism, but it did contain many ideas similar to those of the Fascists. Speaking about the conflict between workers and their employers, Taylor wrote that "the majority of these men believe that the fundamental interests of employés and employers are necessarily antagonistic. Scientific management, on the contrary, has for its very foundation the firm conviction that the true interests of the two are one and the same." Taylor argues that the two classes will come together because "what constitutes a fair day's work will be a question for scientific investigation, instead of a subject to be bargained and haggled over," and that furthermore they will come to know each other better as they work closely together to increase productivity. Although he surely intended nothing like its future political consequences, the literal image of the *fascio*, which inscribed an ideology of the individual at the same time that it celebrated communal solidarity, might have been discerned in Taylor's vision of the future society:

> The time is fast going by for the great personal or individual achievement of any one man standing alone and without the help of those around him. And the time is coming when all great things will be done by that type of cooperation in which each man performs the function for which he is best suited, each man preserves his own individuality and is supreme in his particular function, and each man at the same time loses none of his originality and proper personal initiative, and yet is controlled by and must work harmoniously with many other men.[31]

Any movement as complex as scientific management contains many potential themes, and as Pound sought new ways of understanding social oppression after the First World War, it is not surprising that he responded to a populist rhetoric to which he would have been oblivious ten years earlier. Perhaps the clearest way to see his new-found receptivity to ideas that scientific management had long espoused is to examine one of his sources. In Canto 38, Pound interrupts a denunciation of arms merchants with a passage describing a factory:

> and he, Metevsky said to the other side
> (three children, five abortions and died of the last)
> he said: the other boys got more munitions

(thus cigar-makers whose work is highly repetitive
can perform the necessary operations almost automatically
and at the same time listen to readers who are hired
for the purpose of providing mental entertainment while they
work; Dexter Kimball 1929.)[32]

Dexter S. Kimball was a professor of industrial engineering and dean
of the College of Engineering at Cornell University. He is regarded by
present-day historians as "a prominent progressive engineer during
the 1930's,"[33] and Pound frequently referred to his work, particularly
his 1929 volume, *Industrial Economics*, in reference to topics ranging
from the aesthetics of the machine to railroad bonds. In the "Bibliog-
raphy" section of his "Economic Nature of the United States" (1944),
Pound includes Kimball along with such men as Van Buren and Henry
Adams as authors who must be read: "To get acquainted with the
Technocrats' tendencies Dexter Kimball's *Industrial Economics* would
be useful."[34]

Kimball was a supporter of the scientific management movement,
and his *Industrial Economics* contains extensive summary, and high
praise, of Taylor's contributions to management theory. But his stance
was that of the insider who is nevertheless a critic of some of scientific
management's more humanly destructive aspects. His article, "Another
Side of Efficiency Engineering," had been included in a comprehensive
1914 collection which was intended as a "supplement to the standard
works of Taylor and Gantt." In it, he suggested some of the modifica-
tions which Taylor's theories would undergo during the course of the
1920s and thirties. Kimball affirms the basic aim of increasing industrial efficiency, but he criticizes some of the social consequences of its
application. His often censorious rhetorical style perhaps suggests why
Pound would have found him interesting: "Experience shows that the
rate of pay for industrial workers has not increased in proportion to
the increase in productive capacity; he would indeed be a bold man
who would contend that in our organization today with its immense
burden of high financiers, grafters, drones and incompetents, the
producing classes, including employer and employee, are receiving full
return for the services they render."[35] As in the Italy that Pound would
know a few years later, certain (primarily financial) aspects of capitalism could receive harsh criticism, while employers (silently divorced
from their capitalist roots) and employees were ideologically united
under the rubric of "production."

Kimball argues that scientific management should be used not to
"concentrate labor in the hands of a few," but rather to institute a
"scheme whereby *every* man can be worked up to his full efficiency."
And he takes for granted certain things with which Pound was in full
agreement: "The great problem which confronts us is not and has not
for many years been that of production, but distribution."[36] In an

article in which he refers to Kimball on business failure and the "cycle of crisis," Pound too asserts that "it should be apparent that in this great association there is an enormous source of riches. 'Science has solved the problem of production,' etc."[37] The problem of distribution was central to Pound's own economic schemes, of course, and he reserves the lowest place in his private hell (in Canto 14) for those who would obstruct distribution:

> And Invidia,
> the corruptio, foetor, fungus,
> liquid animals, melted ossifications,
> slow rot, foetid combustion,
>   chewed cigar-butts, without dignity, without tragedy,
> . . . . . m Episcopus, waving a condom full of black-beetles,
> monopolists, obstructors of knowledge,
>   obstructors of distribution.[38]

In Kimball Pound evidently found a voice among the Technocrats which not only seemed to speak against the human costs of modern work—an issue which had been of concern to Pound long before he discovered economic theory—but which reinforced his own economic schemes. Kimball proposes, in *Industrial Economics*, that now that the "*science* of production" is so well advanced, an equivalent effort should be made to study the laws of distribution: "*What is most needed is scientific distribution.*"[39]

Although the populist strain in Taylor's program is more apparent in Kimball than in many of those associated with scientific management, Kimball in no way rejected any of the movement's major programs for control of the workplace. When he proposed that factory workers might be provided with "mental entertainment," for example, he was defending scientific management against what had proven to be a damaging critique, namely, that Taylorism depended upon processes of fragmentation and de-skilling, with a consequent dehumanization of the worker. In *Industrial Economics*, the passage about the cigar makers which Pound quotes verbatim in Canto 38 is introduced as an explicit defense against the charge that workers have been degraded: "Division of labor has been strongly criticized because of the narrowing effect it exercises upon the mentality of the worker when he is required to do repetitive work of a very narrow range."[40] Kimball views these effects as "overestimated," but he does acknowledge that scientific management must confront the issue.

This question, of what was happening to the human subject in the modern workplace, raises an important issue with regard to any attempt to understand a work such as the *Cantos* in its historical context. For many recent critics, the notion of a "unified subject" is taken to be politically and metaphysically wrong, wherever it occurs. For example, Paul Smith argues that "the discoveries of Lacan, via

Freud, of the relations of the individual subject to the network of the symbolic, and metonymy's role in the signification of desire, show that privilege to be based on an illusory plenitude—that of the subject who speaks and knows (what he is saying). No more determined an example of such a subject could be found than the tactless and insistent Ezra, the priest."[41] However, the struggle of a figure like Pound to retain the "illusory plenitude of the subject" should be seen in relation to a social context in which the subject was in fact being drained of its autonomy, in which the fragmentation of mind and hand was an explicit policy of industrial management. Kimball's felt need to qualify his defense of that policy in the face of widespread criticism is an indication that, however unjustified the "unified subject" might be philosophically (and I am not addressing that question), the notion of human wholeness could be a powerful means of cultural resistance for those opposed to the latest schemes for further rationalizing the processes of production.

Pound's quotation from Kimball in Canto 38 raises questions which are similar to those posed by his earlier reference to the Confucian historians who left blanks in their writings. Was he continuing to oppose the technological degradation of the worker, or was he rather closing the issue by means of a populist rhetoric which in fact allowed no space for genuine human difference? Were the workers in the cigar factory actually realizing their full potential of mind as well as body, or were they simply being distracted from the reality of their diminished lives? A few lines after his quotation from Kimball, Pound turns to "the financial aspect" of the factory, launching into a summary of Major Douglas's thesis that there is a clog in the system of distribution because the amount paid out by a factory for wages and dividends never equals the factory's total payments (which include raw materials, interest, etc.). For all the tongue-in-cheek wit of its statement, Pound is perfectly serious about his conclusion:

> and the light became so bright and so blindin'
>   in this layer of paradise
>   that the mind of man was bewildered.[42]

Increasingly, the light which dawns on this Poundian Dante (in the language of men like Major Douglas) seems to come from some absolute source, beyond the reach of ordinary mortals. It is a light which casts no shadows. Earlier, when he was just beginning his long poem, Pound had found in Ernest Fenollosa's pamphlet, *The Chinese Written Character as a Medium for Poetry*, a different view of language. Through the tyranny of a "logic of classification," European civilization seemed to Fenollosa to have sliced and baked thought "into little hard units or concepts." With sentences constructed of these bricks, language came to blind us to that multiplicity of function which nature must possess if it is, as he believed, an infinitely large field of potential interrelationship. Against this language which, factory-like, would narrow and control, Fenollosa sets an ideogrammic model in which "the cherry tree is all that it does." Composed of correlated verbs which "may be almost infinite in number," the ideogram works through a concentration of meanings into itself, *including* multiplicity rather than reducing it to a listing of discrete, purified alternatives. Fenollosa's comparison of the Chinese ideograph to the "blood-stained battle-flags" of an old campaigner is particularly revealing. Bearing layers of meaning accumulated through history, words are more than simply rich and complex. They are the sites of struggle and change as well. For Fenollosa, "all truth has to be expressed in sentences because all truth is the *transference of power*."[43]

Fenollosa's notes only confirmed, however, a theory of language and culture which Pound had already begun working out some years before. In "I Gather the Limbs of Osiris," he had made a distinction between the "symptomatic" author, who simply reflects the styles and modes of thought of a particular historical moment, and the "donative" author, whose function is far more innovative, in a particular way: "But the 'donative' author seems to draw down into the art something which was not in the art of his predecessors. If he also draw from the air about him, he draws latent forces, or things present but unnoticed, or things perhaps taken for granted but never examined."[44] The cultural change initiated by Pound's "donative" author originates not in some primary creation out of nothing, but rather in making manifest those "latent forces" to which society had previously been blinded by its dominant patterns of perception. In his earlier opposition to the hegemony of technocratic discourse in his age, Pound had attempted to represent language as openly contentious and historical, rather than single and inevitable—that is, as containing many possibilities, both latent and dominant. But during the twenties and thirties, as his poetry became (in his own eyes) more explicitly dedicated to disrupting tradition and his rhetoric became more stridently oppositional, his writing, ironically, became more and more symptomatic of the modernity he was attacking. Extending the techniques which *Mauberley* had shown to be so effective in historicizing social discourse, the *Cantos* nevertheless came to reproduce some of the twentieth century's most repressive and exclusionary discourse.

To be sure, there are still traces in the *Cantos* of Pound's earlier view of language as preserving, like a battle-stained banner, the successive forms which men and women have imposed on their history. Sometimes the fragmentation of Pound's poem does support the contention, central to all socially oppositional programs, that the world is indeed open to change. Canto 21, for example, deals with the subject of various kinds of renewal achieved out of discontinuity. The canto interweaves material from several of the poem's areas of major concern: the Italian Renaissance, the early years of the American republic, and Greek mythology. Beginning with very fragmented glimpses of Cosimo di Medici (supporting scholars and artists, and controlling his enemies through the manipulation of credit), the poem moves to a more sustained letter from Thomas Jefferson (seeking to recruit a gardener who could play the French horn), then back to a Medici anecdote, and finally ends with the appearance of several gods and goddesses.

Although the canto's fragments might be seen as figuring some kind of organic wholeness, and thus as centering a stable order characterized by continuity in repetition, the renewal that emerges out of confusion need not be that of sameness reborn, but may instead issue in difference, in a radical reordering of the past. And the "discontinuous" gods of this canto are in fact gods of change and new order.

> In the crisp air,
>   the discontinuous gods;
> Pallas, young owl in the cup of her hand,
> And, by night, the stag runs, and the leopard
> Owl-eye amid pine boughs.
> Moon on the palm-leaf,
>   confusion;
> Confusion, source of renewals; . . .[45]

Dionysus, himself dismembered and devoured, resorts to bloody violence when men refuse to accept his innovations, and yet he is a civilizing deity, protecting the crucial art of viniculture, in which nature is transformed through human effort. Apollo presides over the movement of Greek society out of the old blood ethic and into the new order of Athenian justice and rationality. Like Pallas, he offers human beings the arts of civilization, including archery, medicine, law, and philosophy. At the end of Canto 21, Persephone is carried off by Dis in a violent breach of the old order which ultimately initiates the cycle of seasonal change. Her myth does not begin until the idyll has ended, and it governs a world in which organic renewal is not an absolute, but a sign of the fall into time.

Thus when Cosimo, patronizing philosophy, is set down beside Thomas Jefferson, who seeks to introduce music and vineyards into his new world, the presence of Athena, Apollo, and Dionysus in the poem directs the reader not into some timeless mythic realm, but back into the world of history—as the gods do, in fact, in a work such as *The Oresteia*. As deities presiding over the human transition from nature to culture, these figures authorize a world of work and change. The gold which structures Cosimo's world is the material basis for the elaborate manipulations of credit through which individuals are placed into positions of power and subordination. Lorenzo, like Odysseus, repeatedly extricates himself and his father from dangerous situations by manipulating words. Their world is a dynamic, and therefore highly unstable, balancing of forces set in motion by human will. Thomas Jefferson is portrayed as primarily a builder, gathering together all the crafts necessary to transform his wilderness into a place of civilization. The power to construct new worlds is figured concisely, and literally, by the reference to Pound's own grandfather: "And 'that man sweated blood to put through that railway.'" In building a railroad across Wisconsin, Thaddeus Pound had helped to construct the material lines of communication through which men and women constitute human society. Thus Canto 21 depicts the human power to make the world through work, and it does so through a figure of change and progress which is inscribed in the canto's very fragmentation.

Far more often, though, the openness of Pound's poetic form is closed by a content of ideas as fixed and absolute as the "essential economic law" of scientific management:

> FIVE million youths without jobs
> Four million adult illiterates
> 15 million 'vocational misfits', that is with small chance for jobs
> NINE million persons annual, injured in preventable industrial
> accidents
> One hundred thousand violent crimes. The Eunited States ov
> America
> 3rd year of the reign of F. Roosevelt, signed F. Delano, his uncle.
> CASE for the prosecution.[46]

It is to Pound's credit that issues as prosaic as unemployment and industrial accidents should be included in his poetry. Nevertheless, these things have become a "case"—that is, for Pound, a limited set of indisputable facts—and he assumes the case to be closed.

Technological determinism is an ideological position which would blind us to the fact that the actual forms which work assumes are always negotiable, that they represent the resolution of conflicting interests in ways which may be just or unjust, but which are always political. In *Mauberley*, Pound had begun to experiment with formal techniques which undermined ideologically interested discourses by fracturing the seamless "naturalness" on which they depend. By the *Cantos*, however, the assault on "Usury" had assumed a role as rigidly ideological as that played by any of the aging generals or literary technocrats of the earlier poem:

> The looms are hushed one after another
> ten thousand after ten thousand
> Duccio was not by usura
> Nor was 'La Calunnia' painted.
> Neither Ambrogio Praedis nor Angelico
> had their skill by usura

>Nor St Trophime its cloisters;
>Nor St Hilaire its proportion.
>Usury rusts the man and his chisel
>It destroys the craftsman, destroying craft; . . .[47]

Pound was better informed than any of his contemporaries among the modernists about how craft had been destroyed, whether in the extensive rationalizations which were transforming the publishing industry or in the increasing specialization of education after the German model. After the First World War, however, Pound was caught up in the turmoil of European societies, and in spite of his earlier Vorticist opposition to the Italian Futurist movement, with its celebration of technological dynamism, it was Italian fascism which finally won his assent. Italian Fascist rhetoric was characterized by a peculiar combination of support for the revival of older traditions presumed to have been buried by bourgeois modernity, plus great enthusiasm for the technological transformation of the future. The result was a discourse which seemed to support Pound's own vision of social change, but only if he could reimagine the technological developments he had long attacked as suddenly being of two very different kinds. On the one hand, he could continue to denounce repressive industrial and financial practices which, in his eyes, only served entrenched interests, and which, at the most extreme, could be fixed with the radically reductive label of international Jewish conspiracy.

On the other hand, he needed to discover a redeeming kind of technological social manipulation which could support his vision of the new rebuilding of Italy. The progressive, humanistic rhetoric of writers like Dexter Kimball, with his "revisionary" brand of scientific management, would serve very well indeed. Although this double view of technological change enabled Pound to assent to a social discourse of the most dogmatic sort, its rejection of simple technological determinacy might, ironically, have led him in very different directions. To see technology as essentially contested and political, rather than as obeying some inevitable law of natural causality, could have allowed Pound to ground his *Cantos* in the openness of history. That the poem is finally symptomatic of modernity's persistent tendency to foreclose awareness that history is a human construct, however, is a sign of modernism's failure fully to grasp the liberating insights which it had in fact achieved.

Chapter 3

The Discourse of Knowledge: Historical Change in *Women in Love*

———————— **I** ————————

Critical work, artistic work, and the work of material production all involve particular appropriations of language. These special uses of language within society are not isolated from one another, but rather are mutually implicated. In their continuing, necessary transactions, they inscribe a discourse which continues to act—from factory floor to university classroom—to shape the working lives of men and women. In attempting to understand the enormous complexity of the discursive pattern which came to dominance in the early decades of this century, no example is more challenging than that of D. H. Lawrence. Lawrence was at once the most explicit of the modernists, portraying and denouncing the contemporary transformations of work, knowledge, and subjectivity, and a powerful exemplar of the very discourse which was bringing about those changes. With regard to the specific ways in which this general discourse was deployed, the situation becomes still more complex.

In his preface to *Women in Love*, D. H. Lawrence says that "we are now in a period of crisis," that "the people that can bring forth the new passion, the new idea, this people will endure. Those others, that fix themselves in the old idea, will perish with the new life strangled unborn within them."[1] Lawrence's prophetic tone is not accompanied by any concrete definition of what the "new" might be, as he remains within a rhetoric based upon organic metaphors: "New unfoldings struggle up in torment in him, as buds struggle forth from the midst of a plant." He speaks of the First World War's bitterness as a part of his novel's atmosphere, but the war is only a recent, terrible sign for deeper transformations of the social order. The deadly struggle between an "old," outworn culture—Victorian in its morality, capitalist in its economic relations—and a "new," somehow more natural society is Lawrence's true subject, and he suspends his characters in a space between two worlds, where they suffer the constraints of the outworn order as well as the uncertainty of social experiment. Although much of the struggle takes place at the level of personality, *Women in Love* is most fundamentally a novel of social crisis rather than one of individual self-definition. In varying ways, all the important characters are made to feel that their personal agonies somehow originate in a historical moment of disorder and change.

If the novel's characters experience their world as broken, discontinuous with the past, however, Lawrence supplies an interpretive frame for their story which is very coherent indeed. Specifically, they are shown as responding to a complex of changes entailed by the movement of industrial capitalism into a new stage of technological and managerial efficiency. The chapter entitled "The Industrial Magnate," which tells the story of that change, thus occupies a special place within the novel. As a narrative within a narrative, "The Industrial Magnate" assumes a privileged role within the text as a tale of origins, a governing fiction by means of which we might interpret the historical crisis which is the torment of these characters. At this thematic level of knowledge, the characters' experience of discontinuity is thus shown to be only apparent, as it is recontained by the familiar shape of narrative history. And in formal terms as well, the openness of much of the novel would seem to be contradicted—or resolved—by the closure of this traditional chapter.

To argue that a chapter may be seen to occupy a privileged position such as this, of course, is not to suggest that Lawrence has provided a key to his novel's meaning. The interpretive clarity which this wonderfully coherent narrative of historical change seems to offer the reader is contradicted by nearly everything else in this novel about the terrible difficulty of even understanding, much less accommodating to, this very process of transformation. Lawrence himself, of course, often warned against the dangers of a naive reading which fails to acknowledge the indirections of literary artifice: "The artist usually sets out—or used to—to point a moral and adorn a tale. The tale, however, points the other way, as a rule. Two blankly opposing morals, the artist's and the tale's. Never trust the artist. Trust the tale. The proper function of a critic is to save the tale from the artist who created it."[2] Lawrence is quite firm in his contention that good art "will tell you the truth" of the artist's day, and yet the language of art is dense, shifting, always on the verge of fossilizing into nontruth, always ready to mislead or mystify. The notion is an important one for understanding Lawrence's demanding and suspicious use of language, and critics have come increasingly to see its power. Frank Kermode, for example, speaks of Lawrence's art as "palimpsest-like," as characterized by a kind of "overpainting" which enhances the generally "indeterminate nature of narrative" and so permits "an indefinite range of interpretation."[3] More recently, Michael Ragussis has examined some of the ways in which Lawrence's readers are enlisted in the task of delineating truth and lies in works which share the equivocity of meaning of most kinds of discourse.[4] Acknowledging Lawrence's own "self-critical gesture," Ragussis sees both artist and reader as engaged in saving the text whenever it threatens to escape into a realm of specious Truth, unconstrained by contextuality, which is the contingent but vital ground of any meaningful statement. Lawrence's language is the central focus here, as his struggle with "the subterfuge of art" becomes a test of whether or not he can succeed in continually renewing his vocabulary and his syntax.

Lawrence was certainly engaged in a struggle to prevent any absolute language pointing to its origin in the Word from trapping the vital substance of his own words, and this need to write beyond the fossil forms of Truth determines one pole of the reader's dilemma in confronting works of great interpretive difficulty. But the difficulties of inventing a language of renewal were set against Lawrence's equal difficulty in telling the truth of his times by constructing a story made out of history. Part of the problematic quality of *Women in Love* lies in the fact that its historical thesis is made so explicit in a subnarrative which at the same time opens history to serious question. In addition to the indeterminacy of language in the novel there is what might be termed an indeterminacy of history, if history is regarded as existing in the space between social event and storytelling.

This problem of how historical narratives function within a context of social change is not unique to Lawrence's fiction. Victor Turner, for example, has studied similar problems of social representation in other cultures, and some of his terms may be helpful in this instance. Turner argues that the genealogy of literary narrative begins in what he calls "social dramas," public breaches of social norms or rules of morality which are understood to express deeper divisions within a society and which must issue in some redress or reordering of the "components of a social field." Several important conditions exist in these social dramas, and they remain embedded in the later forms (such as juridical procedures and literary narrative) which derive from them. First, liminality is always present: we are witnessing a breach between conflicting interests and forms of social order, and whatever the resolution, "a momentous juncture or turning point" in the life of the society will have been passed. The process is characterized by an essential indeterminacy, however, because "indeterminacy is, so to speak, in the subjunctive mood, since it is that which is not yet settled, concluded, and known. It is all that may be, might be, could be, perhaps even should be."[5]

Thus we are dealing with a passage from one social order to another, a process of social change which is indeterminate insofar as it has not yet been determined and so may be characterized by its openness, its potentiality. Another kind of openness enters when social drama is reenacted as ritual or narrative. As performance within history, this reinscribing is subject to new conflict and need, and so may itself change, generating "precedents" which are in fact unprecedented. This second openness, which in literary terms is the indeterminacy of rewriting, is central to an aspect of narrative which demands particular care on the part of critics. A narrative may, on the one hand, inscribe a social passage as paradigmatic, or normative: in Turner's terms, it may serve as a "model of," validating and reinforcing a particular social condition. But it may equally well serve as "model for," initiating change in the order of society rather than reproducing the forms of the past.

I have described Turner's argument at some length because I believe that it generates precisely the kinds of questions which need to be asked about the use of history in fiction, such as Lawrence's, which situates itself so explicitly within a process of social conflict and transformation. If we are dealing with a narrative which treats some crucial juncture within history, we may ask what specific structure and meaning the passage from one social state to another is made to assume in its narrative form. What kind of resolution is enabled? Would an archaeology of a text such as *Women in Love* reveal that a social process which is characterized by indeterminacy and potentiality at some points has been made to appear closed and natural at others? To what extent is the reader to assume that any narrative is a "model of" history, recounting a reality which must be accepted because "true"? When is it, in part at least, a "model for," a rewriting of history which is itself an intervention in the continuous play of social power? The rhetoric of Lawrence's fiction claims to practice both kinds of narrative, and while I would argue that both are in fact bound up with social meaning and power, it is useful to distinguish between Lawrence the analyst of present-day social reality and Lawrence the prophet of a future which has not yet come to pass. As Christopher Caudwell pointed out many years ago, one of the great problems of Lawrence's writing is that the prophet largely ignores the insights of the social critic.[6]

II

Women in Love places its characters in the bewildering space of a radically changing world. "The Industrial Magnate" tells the story of how that change came about through the succession of generations, a story which has at its center the social drama of Gerald Crich and his father. There is a long-standing, unspoken enmity between these two men, and when power is finally handed on and Thomas Crich accepts his retirement, both father and son understand that the transition over which they preside is not simply a personal one. The older man had lived his life in accordance with the dominant nineteenth-century pattern of social and economic order. A patriarch in industrial and domestic settings alike, he imagined there to be no great distance between himself and his workers, largely trusting their skill and experience to extract the resources which would provide a more abundant life for all. His own role was that of benevolent overseer, guided by Christian charity, assuring the well-being of those men and women whose subservient position made them his responsibility. The order which Gerald initiates is very different indeed. Following the notion that business should concern itself with profit, and not charity, he installs what Lawrence terms "the great reform":

> Expert engineers were introduced in every department. An enormous electric plant was installed, both for lighting and for haulage underground, and for power. The electricity was carried into every mine. New machinery was brought from America, such as the miners had never seen before, great iron men, as the cutting machines were called, and unusual appliances. The working of the pits was thoroughly changed, all the control was taken out of the hands of the miners, the butty system was abolished. Everything was run on the most accurate and delicate scientific method, educated and expert men were in control everywhere, the miners were reduced to mere mechanical instruments. They had to work hard, much harder than before, the work was terrible and heart-breaking in its mechanicalness.[7]

Although this is an account of the reorganization of work within a single industry, its features are representative of the general movement in early twentieth-century society which I outlined in my introductory chapter. To be sure, the Taylorism which had been at the forefront of the movement to rationalize the workplace in the United States (and in the other industrialized nations of Western Europe, as well as the Soviet Union) was more bitterly resisted by British labor than by American, and management too was wary of this new instance of Americanization. Nevertheless, such resistance did not mean that England was a place apart from the larger discursive transformations, with all their attendant social consequences, which Taylor had begun to regularize, publicize, and apply to specific industrial situations.[8]

Several details in the account of Gerald's new program are particularly significant. First of all, though the introduction of powerful new machinery is hardly surprising, this development is linked with several others. Expert engineers are introduced, and while their apparent function is to oversee the new technology, they enable another development far more crucial to the new organization of production: the withdrawal of control over their work from the men in the pits. The "butty system," for example, was a kind of subcontracting in which experienced miners were responsible for hiring and paying their own immediate workmates.[9] As we saw earlier, in the account of his earlier experiments in the systematic study of management, Frederick Taylor explicitly argued that nineteenth-century management could not increase its power as long as it allowed workers to retain control over the knowledge upon which industrial processes depend. By appropriating knowledge as its own exclusive function, distinct from and superior to practical execution, management could assume an entirely new level of effective control.[10]

Lawrence seems to be as fully aware as any contemporary student of Taylor's scientific management that a fundamental shift of power was occurring, and that its necessary agents were the educated and expert men who "were in control everywhere." The "most accurate and delicate scientific method" was the final arbiter, not only authorizing the power of a new class of managers, but effecting a radical division of work itself into that of mind and that of hand.[11] The further degradation of industrial labor which Lawrence describes was one consequence of the split, but he also notes that "a highly educated man costs very little more than a workman," and that as the men become mere instruments even Gerald the owner finds himself reduced to a "supreme instrument of control." In concluding that "the mines were nothing but the clumsy efforts of impure minds,"[12] and that mankind was "pure instrumentality," Gerald embraces a "systems approach" entirely congruent with the "information society" and its search for artificial intelligence which characterizes late twentieth-century society. Although he retains the considerable material benefits of ownership, Gerald experiences a loss of autonomy like that of the men, as an apparently objective logic of systems, rather than individual will, comes to govern the processes of production.

The patterns I have pointed out in Lawrence's description may be found in any standard account of early twentieth-century industrial change. His critique of the process he has described in these straightforward terms is also well known. It turns most fundamentally on the opposition, organic/mechanical: "It was the first great step in undoing, the first great phase of chaos, the substitution of the mechanical principle for the organic, the destruction of the organic purpose, the organic unity, and the subordination of every organic unit to the great mechanical purpose. It was pure organic disintegration and pure mechanical organisation. This is the first and finest state of chaos."[13] Gerald and his men, though embracing mechanism in very different ways, are all implicated in the loss of living, purposeful order. That vital order is set over against a mechanical organization which is, paradoxically, not order at all, but chaos, because it flattens individuality in its relentless structure of equality and repetition. This critique runs throughout the novel, as, for example, in the scene in which Birkin and Ursula buy and then give away an old chair. Birkin's contention that the chair still expresses thought, in contrast to the "foul mechanicalness" of present-day production, is consistent with the view of Gerald's new order as dependent on a radical separation and hierarchization of hand and mind.

In denouncing the reduction of men and women to the status of cogs in a machine, however, Lawrence does not simply romanticize the past. If the workers were less constrained before Gerald's "reforms," they were nevertheless subject to a system of control which is unmasked only when the lock-out forces a confrontation between master and men. Coming hat in hand to receive old Mr. Crich's charity, the workers were playing their part in an economy governed by the image of Christ humbling himself in the service of mankind. Believing "that in Christ he was one with his workmen," Mr. Crich is actually shown (through the eyes of his wife) to be indulging in a necessarily hierarchical relation of master and servant, "as if her husband were some subtle funeral bird, feeding on the miseries of the people." This dark side of charity is eliminated by Gerald when he rejects the provision of widow's coal, a practice based on the illusion (vital to his father) that the family firm is indeed an institution of charity. In rejecting his father's desire to be one in Christ with his men, however, Gerald yearns for a divine presence which is equally destructive in Lawrence's eyes: "the desire to translate the Godhead into pure mechanism."[14] Gerald's merger with the God in the machine stands in Lawrence's critique as the final, fraudulent authorization of mechanism's triumph over the vital ineffability of true divinity.

III

Lawrence's novel presents itself to the reader as the exploration of a discourse of opposition, the difficult struggle to forge a language of life rather than mechanical death. History is essential to this stance because it constitutes the supposed ground of reality which justifies the author's prophetic voice as well as the urgency of his characters' struggles. But though Lawrence's presentation and critique of the direction of contemporary social change seems familiar enough, even "natural" at this point, some of its key terms are highly problematic. If the succession of Gerald Crich to his father's power figures most concretely the larger transformation of society which is the novel's subject, this interrelation of father and son is part of a still more inclusive concern of Lawrence's with old and new.

The American struggle to forge an identity apart from its European origins offered an example of great historical importance for Lawrence, who read in it a pattern very similar to the one which he created for the Crich family. In *Studies in Classic American Literature*, he identifies America's failure to break free with its preeminence as a technological power: "All this Americanizing and mechanizing has been for the purpose of overthrowing the past. And now look at America, tangled in her own barbed wire, and mastered by her own machines. Absolutely got down by her own barbed wire of shalt-nots, and shut up fast in her own 'productive' machines like millions of squirrels running in millions of cages."[15] Lawrence characterizes the American response as a "rebellion against the old parenthood of Europe," and this generational figure for social change (as in the instance of Gerald and his father) operates within a metaphor which runs through much of Lawrence's writing during these years. His metaphor of the tree, and more specifically of the tree's "leading-shoot," as a figure for human life, in "The Study of Thomas Hardy," is particularly revealing:

> It seems to me as if a man, in his normal state, were like a palpitating leading-shoot of life, where the unknown, all unresolved, beats and pulses, containing the quick of all experiences, as yet unrevealed, not singled out. But when he thinks, when he moves, he is retracing some proved experience. He is as the leading-shoot which, for the moment, remembers only that which is behind, the fixed wood, the cells conducting toward their undifferentiated tissue of life. He moves as it were in the trunk of the tree, in the channels long since built, where the sap must flow as in a canal. He takes knowledge of all this past experience upon which the new tip rides quivering, he becomes again the old life, which has built itself out in the fixed tissue, he lies in line with the old movement, unconscious of where it breaks, at the growing plasm, into something new, unknown.[16]

Here the contrast between new and old becomes one of living shoot set against the fixed matter of previously defined cells. Only the undifferentiated tip is acknowledged to possess life, while the trunk out of which it grows is "fixed wood," a "canal," little more than old lumber. To think is always a "retracing," a turning back from life, which is essentially unconscious. Knowledge is therefore limited to the rigid structures of the past, and can play no part in the mysterious being of life.

Throughout *Women in Love* this knowledge which turns away from life is a key site of struggle for all the lovers. Hermione and Ursula repeatedly seek to "know" Birkin, and he resists with a kind of vague horror that his vitality would be threatened by their knowledge. Gudrun is "like Eve reaching to the apples on the tree of knowledge" as she kisses Gerald. Her desire to "touch him, till she had him all in her hands, till she had strained him into her knowledge,"[17] brings death with it as surely as Eve's mythic apples. As a medium through which the interpersonal struggles of these characters are played out, knowledge represents the acceptance of fixed, imprisoning structures of personality, in contrast to the dangerous, unknowable vitality of true self-definition. The notion that reason is a threat to vitality and spontaneity remains a powerful one, as the pop psychology of any grocery store magazine rack will quickly testify. But while this struggle for personal salvation may be viewed as a psychological and metaphysical conflict, it remains rooted in a crisis of social change, both in the novel's narrative frame and in the details of its metaphoric patterns.

In elaborating his figure of the tree, Lawrence describes the man who turns away from the living tip as "happy" where "all is known, all is finite, all is established, and knowledge can be perfect here in the trunk of the tree, which life built up and climbed beyond." But consider the statement which follows these words: "such is a man at work." In Lawrence's formulation, the fixed cells and rigid channels of the tree trunk are equated with the mechanistic quality of modern work. If the cells of old wood signify nothing more than the retracing of past movements, man working is equally the image of fruitless repetition: "A man who can repeat certain movements accurately is an expert, if his movements are those which produce the required result. And these movements are the calculative or scientific movements of a machine. When a man is working perfectly, he is the perfect machine." When Gerald experiences his vision of what he might accomplish with his newly gained control of the firm, his terms are precisely the same: "And for this fight with matter one must have perfect instruments in perfect organisation, a mechanism so subtle and harmonious in its workings that it represents the single mind of man, and by its relentless repetition of given movement, will accomplish a purpose irresistibly, inhumanly."[18] Thus, in social terms, the mechanistic repetition of modern work replicates the fixed sameness of cells which no longer contain life.

At the heart of Lawrence's social critique there is the metaphor of the organism: "the destruction of the organic purpose, the organic unity, and the subordination of every organic unit to the great mechanical purpose."[19] But Lawrence's recurring figure requires us to accept a rather troubling paradox. The vital tip of emergent life is set against its contrary, the fixed channels (mechanism) of the dead trunk. And yet trunk and tip are one organism, the living shoot depending absolutely on the branch which supports it. Whether explicit or submerged, these contradictory implications of the organic metaphor are widespread in Lawrence's writing. Consider, for example, Birkin's revulsion against speech, which would trap him in the fixed cells of the already-said. He seeks a language beyond the imprisoning old forms, and yet, even the most exploratory act of language, like a "leading-shoot," is inseparable from the fixed structures, the grammar, of past utterance.

What are the consequences of this figure which is so pervasive, and so contradictory, in Lawrence's thought? This is Birkin, struggling to find his new language: "There was always confusion in speech. Yet it must be spoken. Whichever way one moved, if one were to move forwards, one must break a way through. And to know, to give utterance, was to break a way through the walls of the prison as the infant in labour strives through the walls of the womb." Prison or no, the womb of old speech must be acknowledged as an unavoidable necessity. Nor is our physical survival any less dependent on work, however mechanistic and life-denying. This is how Lawrence puts it in "The Study of Thomas Hardy": "Work is, simply, the activity necessary for the production of a sufficient supply of food and shelter: nothing more holy than that. It is the producing of the means of self-preservation. Therefore it is obvious that it is not the be-all and the end-all of existence. We work to provide means of subsistence, and when we have made subsistence, we proceed to live."[20]

What is most revealing about Lawrence's equations of tree with mechanism, and womb with prison, is the way these images allow him to distance the realm of fixed cell/mechanism/dead speech. Since the presentation of this realm is governed by the various forms of the organic metaphor, it appears to be natural and thus inevitable, and as a consequence the mechanical seems to exist in a kind of isolated state prior to any meaningful contention within society. Thus Lawrence can argue, with all the zeal of Frederick Taylor himself, that a man's movements in work (whether he be doctor, lawyer, or mechanic) should approximate "the calculative or scientific movements of a machine." It follows then that whatever new techniques are capable of increasing industrial productivity should be employed, because work falls entirely within the sphere of practical necessity and has little or nothing to do with the real struggle for human salvation. By taking this view of work, Lawrence the vitalist ends up in agreement with his mechanistic enemies.

Thus Birkin, in his quarreling with Gerald over the value of material production, shows no interest in what Gerald actually does to increase that production. He focuses instead only on the "higher" questions which can be asked after the coal has been dug and the rabbits stewed. Insofar as Birkin is a mouthpiece for Lawrence's critique of recent social change, however, his message is largely consistent with the traditional assumptions of British management. For the most part, managers in Britain were not expected to interest themselves in engineering issues, but rather to practice a style of management which Judith A. Merkle has characterized as "moral leadership and technical ignorance."[21] This style of management was rooted in a complex system of social class traditions, particularly the long-standing hostility on the part of British aristocracy toward those engaged in business and industry, and the corresponding desire of the rising industrialists to share in the cultural prestige of the aristocrat. The cultural assumptions of this system of social hierarchy made British managers fearful of being identified as technocrats, with the result that scientific management had more difficulty in being openly accepted in Britain than elsewhere in Europe and North America.

In Lawrence's novel, Gerald does apply many of Taylor's basic principles to the workings of his mines, and his identity (social as well as personal) seems to be fatally undermined as a result of this embrace of mechanistic thought. It is for Birkin, in his affirmation of "higher matters," to reflect not only the more typical attitude of British managers, but an important contradiction in Lawrence's own position. In basing his critique of Gerald's innovations on a hierarchy subordinating work to consciousness, Birkin was unwittingly repeating a strategy crucial to the program of scientific management. If work were to be rationalized as Taylor hoped, then a radical division between mind and hand would first have to be instituted, with knowledge withdrawn from the shop floor and installed in a separate, and superior, realm of management expertise. Furthermore, knowledge itself would have to be redefined along strictly instrumental lines.

With regard to the status of knowledge, Lawrence's metaphor of the growing tip of the tree branch as mystery and the unspoken, in contradistinction to knowing, which he associates with dead wood and mechanistic repetition, is particularly important. Like work, Lawrence consigns knowledge to the realm of the merely instrumental.[22] This instrumentalization of knowledge was essential to the reorganization of work in Europe and America which was taking place during the first two decades of the twentieth century, and it is in fact described by Lawrence as central to Gerald's reordering of the mines. The "experts" who have placed knowledge at Gerald's disposal as a powerful new agency of industrial control have at the same time effectively withdrawn knowledge from the workers, who may henceforth function mechanically according to procedures worked out elsewhere. By ceding knowledge to the sphere of the mechanistic and the pragmatic, Lawrence has powerfully reinforced the very movement within society which, at the same time, he denounces as destructive of "organic unity." Thus there is a counterargument within Lawrence's writing at this time which is surprisingly congruent with contemporary traditions of genteel management, and which precisely contradicts "The Industrial Magnate's" overt narrative of a world made less and less receptive to genuine life by the growing power of mechanistic thought.

IV

In the account of Gerald's great transformation of the mines, the response of the men themselves poses a number of questions. After describing their new work as "terrible and heart-breaking in its mechanicalness," Lawrence writes, "But they submitted to it all. The joy went out of their lives, the hope seemed to perish as they became more and more mechanised. And yet they accepted the new conditions. They even got a further satisfaction out of them."[23] In his description of the worker's perception of these new ways of organizing work, Lawrence echoes what was in fact the overwhelming response of the British unions, which (like the traditional management class, though for different reasons) were unvarying in their hostility to anything remotely suggestive of Taylorism.[24] And yet in spite of their perception of the changes as overwhelmingly negative, Lawrence's narrative portrays the men as actually accepting these new conditions which are so oppressive, which at first had even led them to consider murdering Gerald. The suggestion seems to be that it is somehow in the nature of the workers to accept, that the mechanicalness of their work meets a need which is deep within them: "But as time went on, they accepted everything with fatal satisfaction. Gerald was their high priest, he represented the religion they really felt. His father was forgotten already. There was a new world, a new order, strict, terrible, inhuman, but satisfying in its very destructiveness. The men were satisfied to belong to the great and wonderful machine, even whilst it destroyed them."[25]

If it could be argued that there is something in the nature of these men which Gerald's new order touches, it is nevertheless the case that under Gerald's father they felt themselves to be very different. In the older man's world of Christ made flesh, the miners had come to regard themselves as equal in the sight of God, and they eventually used that belief to challenge the great disparity between their earthly state and that of the owners. When Gerald takes control of the firm, the men learn to regard themselves in a way which is not simply new, but which has the effect of accommodating them to the changed conditions of their work. One explanation for this new attitude among the men is that their instincts have become perverted as a result of Gerald's corruption, that they are enacting Nietzsche's vision of cultural decadence.[26] However, the fact that the men have assumed two very different ways of acting and understanding their actions, within the space of a brief narrative, suggests rather that their identities have been redefined by powerful forces within their society.

Under the rubric of "socialization," such forces have been studied by social scientists for many years, of course, though in ways which tend to accept the social norms and concern themselves only with how those norms are inculcated and enforced. "Ideology" would be more likely to suggest the political nature of the process by which men and women are shaped by their society, but regardless of the terminology, the point is that individuals need not be forced to accept dominant social values and patterns of behavior. The assent of the miners to Gerald's new order illustrates what Foucault means by a "disciplinary" society, in which institutional practices, rather than public spectacles such as floggings or hangings, regulate behavior. And contrary to commonly held belief that labor generally opposed the scientific rationalization of industry, Lawrence's depiction of the miners' assent is historically accurate. According to David F. Noble, the "widespread notion" of labor opposition "is fundamentally mistaken . . . so far as twentieth-century workers are concerned. For, like those in management and academia, labor has swallowed whole and internalized the liberal ideology of progress."[27]

As a novel about historical change, *Women in Love* identifies the social crisis which its characters are experiencing with a movement of industrial capitalism to new levels of complexity in its management practice, its increasing dependence on science, and its manner of employing labor. Lawrence in no way presents Gerald as the author of his innovations, but only as the agent of their introduction, as he imports machines from America and hires the expertise of engineers. Though Lawrence never obscures the fact that Gerald gains materially from the changes he initiates, he depicts Gerald as ultimately possessed and destroyed by them. We might well include the master in the question I have posed with regard to the men: Why do they assent?

The answer is that the society shown in Lawrence's narrative is not a society in decadence, but rather a society being taken over by a powerful new version of technological discourse, a version powerful enough to bind individuals at all levels of society. The men are happy to be part of a "great and wonderful machine" which represents "the highest that man had produced." It is perceived as "perfect system" based on "pure mathematical principles." Gerald's terms are essentially the same: "a great and perfect machine, a system," the search for "perfect co-ordination," the translation of "the mystic word harmony into the practical word organisation."[28] This is the discourse of instrumental knowledge, and it structures itself around several key points: an evolutionary metaphor of ever "higher" levels of invention; the elevation of mathematics to a normative role in the judgment of social organization; a validation of the "systems approach" to knowledge as well as practice. The continuing power of this discourse for the twentieth century is suggested by a proposal by Herbert A. Simon (one of the fathers of artificial intelligence, and a theoretician of "management science") to displace humanistic study as the center of liberal education. He wrote, in 1969, "The proper study of mankind has been said to be man. But I have argued that man—or at least the intellective component of man—may be relatively simple; that most of the complexity of his behavior may be drawn from his environment, from his search for good designs. If I have made my case, then we can conclude that, in large part, the proper study of mankind is the science of design, not only as the professional component of a technical education but as a core discipline for every liberally educated man."[29]

To install the science of design at the center of liberal education would simply be to complete the institutionalization of a process which Lawrence saw beginning fifty years earlier. *Women in Love*, like much of his writing, is about men and women who, confronted by this turn in history, succumb to it or seek to resist its power. Lawrence creates men and women who rail against the inroads of the mechanistic, and he locates his fiction within the frame of a coherent historical narrative which seems to be offered as a "model of" that reality against which his characters struggle. But Lawrence's narrative is not a simple representation of history. It is rather an enactment of history which moves in fundamental ways against its own overt message. If the miners assent to become interchangeable parts in a machine, they do so not because Gerald has the power to force them to, but because they, and he, have been constituted by a discourse which makes their assent natural and meaningful. And Lawrence's text is a part of that discourse, reproducing it while at the same time groping for some way to counter it.

For Lawrence's discourse of organicism takes place within, not outside, the discourse of modern mechanization—or rather, both discourses are part of an interrelated complex, not opposites as we tend to think of them. Like the earlier generations of Romantics, Lawrence denounced the machine and used organic metaphor to celebrate life. In doing so, however, he disabled his own counterdiscourse. Against a discursive sphere in which "organization" is a term yielding power, while "harmony" is a concept that can only serve to disqualify and subjugate, Lawrence consigns himself to silence by surrendering knowledge to the realm of the instrumental. In doing so he participates in what Gerald Graff has called the "skepticism toward reason" which has been so prominent a response to industrialization.[30] Birkin may struggle to articulate a new being capable of defying the mechanistic world which surrounds him, but he dooms his project to the status of an irrelevant and outworn humanism by accepting the most crucial terms of Gerald's new order.

But even Gerald is expendable in that order, which defines its power through the very gesture that Lawrence himself makes in dividing the vital and the material, the leading-shoot from the solid wood which supports it. For Lawrence, inchoate life, in all its promise and vitality, is set against the fixity of mechanical production. But for all too many of his contemporaries, that dichotomy had already received a new and unquestionable meaning: trivial mysticism exists on sufferance at the hands of the only meaningful kind of knowledge, knowledge as power. And it is that premise, defining knowledge as instrumental power, which founds the social and economic order of advanced industrial societies in the twentieth century.

Chapter 4

The Self in Lawrence:
Languages of History or Myth

I

Among the great modernist writers, it was D. H. Lawrence who offered the most vividly realized portrait of the human costs involved in the industrialization of work which was proceeding everywhere in his world. He understood that the appropriation of knowledge as instrumental power by industry and by government was essential to the new order of machine production, which required new strategies of management and a work force shaped to new demands. But if Lawrence's voice was loud against this new order, we saw in the last chapter that his resistance to it assumed a form which has made him a curiously problematic figure. Although he was not entirely consistent, the main direction of his arguments and certainly the rhetorical texture of his writings served to reinforce the very discourse which was transforming the lives of his generation. Lawrence saw fixed ideas as the dead husks of life which had already passed on in restless, necessary growth. And all too often he followed that organic metaphor into a rejection of all knowledge, a mystical vitalism which ceded to the managers of the new order precisely the ideology on which their power was based: that knowledge is the province of specialists who confirm its value and power by using it as a problem-solving device which will produce abundance for all.

Knowledge was a key site for the struggle which Lawrence had joined, but not to the point of exhausting the complex play of form and meaning within his works. It is necessary to move beyond Lawrence's specific treatment of knowledge to explore the larger pattern of opposition which he was attempting to establish. In ceding knowledge as instrumental mechanism to the realm of material production, what alternative did he claim in its place? The answer should be familiar after decades of commentary on the modernist tradition by critics working within the paradigm of "spatial form." Whether couched in organic or religious terms, the refuge from modern disorder and decline is always a timeless, mythic realm. And Lawrence's vision has been read in this way through many hundreds of pages of literary criticism. Before examining his own version of abstract star-balance or primitive darkness, however, I would like to turn again to the question of modernist form, and particularly to the ways in which the unsettling openness of that form has so often been recontained by new interpretive closure.

Although Lawrence is generally considered to be one of the major figures of high modernism, his membership in that company is disputed, being equally seen as almost perfectly representative or as only partial and highly qualified. David Lodge, for example, groups him with writers who exhibit only some features of modernism, or exhibit them in modified ways, while Frank Kermode calls *Women in Love* "close to the essence of the modern."[1] As might be expected, even those who agree that Lawrence is a thorough modernist describe the features of his modernism in various ways. Frank Kermode argues that it is the "fluidity" and the "unpredictable tonalities" of *Women in Love* which makes that book so characteristically modern, while for Robert Langbaum "*The Rainbow's* technical innovation is the switch from presented action to analytical narration."[2] And writing from the point of view of Marxist criticism, Terry Eagleton underlines the "break to synchronic form" which he sees in *Women in Love*: "yet it is precisely in its fissuring of organic form, in its 'montage' techniques of symbolic juxtaposition, that the novel enforces a 'progressive' discontinuity with a realist lineage already put into profound question by *Jude the Obscure*."[3] I have already emphasized the importance to modernist practice of discontinuous form, and that feature appears again and again through critical statements such as the above, regardless of their very different terminologies. The "switch from presented action to analytical narration" recognizes the same shattering of the older illusion of formal wholeness as does the notion of a "fissuring of organic form." For Kermode, Lawrence's major works are also characterized by their formal discontinuities: "Far from holding one note, *The Rainbow* is distinguished for its tonal variety"; while in *Women in Love* "there is often little obvious causal connection between the parts; each chapter forms a whole and may often be read out of its proper order or omitted without damage to the narrative line."[4]

This brief catalog of interpretations may seem to be a question of comparing apples and oranges, suggesting as it does discontinuities created by tonal variety, narrative voice, structural montage, and organization by self-sustaining, rearrangeable chapters. In each of these formulations, however, the text is shown to be fissured in specific, though different, ways. In the previous chapter, I suggested a way in which Lawrence embedded one kind of writing within another. "The Industrial Magnate" is a good example of a chapter which could easily stand alone, and part of the reason is that it assumes the familiar language of objective historical narrative. That language is of course very different from the highly metaphoric evocations of a chapter such as "Excurse": "It was the strange mystery of his life-motion, there, at the back of the thighs, down the flanks. It was a strange reality of his being, the very stuff of being, there in the straight downflow of the thighs. It was here she discovered him one of the sons of God such as were in the beginning of the world, not a man, something other, something more."[5] Or, against the repetitive, almost incantatory rhythms of this passage, we might set the socially satiric dialogue of "Creme de Menthe":

> "Do you know London well?"
> "I can hardly say," he laughed. "I've been up a good many times, but I was never in this place before."
> "You're not an artist then?" she said, in a tone that placed him an outsider.
> "No," he replied.
> "He's a soldier, and an explorer, and a Napolean of industry," said Birkin, giving Gerald his credentials for Bohemia. (56f.)

Each of these chapters displays a particular style and carries its own social and philosophical connotations, and each could be used as a norm for reading all the others. Cafe wit and cynicism could certainly puncture the pretentiousness of Ursula's discovery of a son of God (by examining Birkin's thighs), while her language of visionary ecstasy might as easily stand as a critique of the shallowness of fashionable bohemia.

A chapter such as "The Industrial Magnate" does seem to invite just such use, with its limited story of history as origin and end for the uncertainties unfolding in surrounding chapters. This kind of discontinuity, in which the style of one chapter is played off against that of another, may seem less radical than similar techniques in Joyce's fiction or Pound's verse, where the point is often made by the very appearance of the text on the page. Unlike Pound's startling juxtapositions of Provençal and cranky Old West slang, Lawrence's writing is easier to imagine as coherent, unified, and fully identified with its author. But the technique of using multiple styles, each grounded in a specific aspect of modern social history, is pervasive and fundamental to Lawrence's use of language, and it is central to his practice as a modernist artist.

The most helpful terminology for dealing with this difficult but crucial aspect of Lawrence's writing is probably that of M. M. Bakhtin. Bakhtin refuses to remove language from its social context, an operation which would permit us to imagine that language is ideal and unitary. He argues instead that language is always characterized by "centrifugal" and "centripetal" forces in mutual opposition—the one tending to change, diversify, and subvert, while the other seeks to limit and control language's meaning and use. Employing the term "heteroglossia" to describe this manyness of language which is always set against the illusion of One language, coherent and unchanging, Bakhtin emphasizes the concrete social grounding of those multiple dialects which undermine unity:

> But the centripetal forces of the life of language, embodied in a "unitary language," operate in the midst of heteroglossia. At any given moment of its evolution, language is stratified not only into linguistic dialects in the strict sense of the word (according to formal linguistic markers, especially phonetic), but also—and for us this is the essential point—into languages that are socio-ideological: languages of social groups, "professional" and "generic" languages, languages of generations and so forth. From this point of view, literary language itself is only one of these heteroglot languages—and in its turn is also stratified into languages (generic, period-bound and others).[6]

The linguistic stratification which Bakhtin describes is not simply an abstract feature of language and literature but a highly significant social phenomenon. The play of sublanguages within a text reveals one of the ways in which the various groups within society define themselves and assume positions of mutual relationship. The social order within which this process occurs is always a dynamic one, in which dominant groups seek to fix the language which sanctions their power and identity, while those who are excluded preserve the diversity of their own languages in resistance to the domination of a single Truth.

Bakhtin's argument does not simply point out difference as it exists between large units presumed to be relatively coherent within themselves (e.g., Québecois, ghetto slang). Rather, it assumes that heteroglossia is embedded everywhere in language, even in individual words, which may bear the most contradictory senses. In this acceptance (which is shared by all modern linguists) of difference as a basic linguistic principle, Bakhtin's position might seem to resemble that of deconstruction, but its premises, as well as its practical consequences for criticism, are very different indeed. While deconstructionists use the notion of difference to construct a metaphysical argument, alleging that difference is universally present because it is of the essence of Language itself, Bakhtin sees linguistic difference as the sign that languages are fundamentally social, that they are the record of historical order, contention, and change. Focusing on particular language performances, rather than on the abstraction, Language, Bakhtin insists that any utterance, or written text, must be understood in relation to the historical conditions of its production. If language is always potentially open to change, because of its inherent heteroglossia, it is also always closed because every linguistic act is the act of a specific man or woman in a specific historical situation.

In Bakhtin's view, the rise of the novel has been particularly important in teaching us to see the historical contentiousness of language:

> The novel is the expression of a Galilean perception of language, one that denies the absolutism of a single and unitary language—that is, that refuses to acknowledge its own language as the sole verbal and semantic center of the ideological world. It is a perception that has been made conscious of the vast plenitude of national and, more to the point, social languages—all of which are equally capable of being "languages of truth," but, since such is the case, all of which are equally relative, reified and limited, as they are merely the languages of social groups, professions and other cross-sections of everyday life. The novel begins by presuming a verbal and semantic decentering of the ideological world, a certain linguistic homelessness of literary consciousness, which no longer possesses a sacrosanct and unitary linguistic medium for containing ideological thought.[7]

For Bakhtin, the novel's power to display the verbal decentering which it presumes is located in its "dialogic" nature. Incorporating many languages into itself, the novel speaks with two voices—that of the author and that of the particular language which is being represented at any given moment. What is decentered is not all meaning or all language, however, but "the ideological world." Such a decentering, with its resultant "homelessness," is not a metaphysical event but a political one. All that has been lost is the "sacrosanct" status of ideology—that is, its apparent naturalness, its inevitability.

II

If Lawrence's use of a variety of conflicting styles does accomplish the sort of decentering which Bakhtin describes, the result is not therefore a novel about "decentering." The kind of sacrosanct, ideological discourse that might actually be decentered by a novel such as *Women in Love* depends on the specific historical conditions in which it was written and read. That is, the question is not whether heteroglossia was potentially available to Lawrence, but what use he

made of it—whether to reinforce a particular unitary language, that
of instrumental reason, for example, or on the contrary to reveal the
historical contingency of all social discourse.

If we would understand Lawrence's opposition, on the level of
language, to the mechanism and instrumentality of the modern
industrialized world, *The Rainbow* must be read along with *Women in
Love*. At the beginning of *The Rainbow*, Lawrence makes a distinction
between the men of the Marsh, who move through the seasons in a
kind of unconsciousness, close to nature, and the women, who yearn
for the larger world of human society: "But the women looked out
from the heated, blind intercourse of farm life, to the spoken world
beyond. They were aware of the lips and the mind of the world
speaking and giving utterance, they heard the sound in the distance,
and they strained to listen."[8] The mute life of the farm is not
Lawrence's ideal, posed in opposition to the corrupt world of town and
factory. But it does remain a significant connection to the older world
of human wholeness which must be recovered and then made over
into the pattern for a radically new future. To figure that natural life as
mute, and the world beyond the farm as "spoken," is characteristic of
Lawrence. He pictures the woman as desiring "to see what man had
done in fighting outwards to knowledge" and straining "to hear how he
uttered himself." And the public world of the town does utter itself very
fully in these novels, as Lawrence gives us the speech of schoolmasters
and artists and mine owners.

But he also gives us the dark, "natural" world of the elder
Tom—and this supposedly speechless world must also be represented
in words: "The reality of her who was just beyond him absorbed him.
Blind and destroyed, he pressed forward, nearer, nearer, to receive the
consummation of himself, he received within the darkness which
should swallow him and yield him up to himself. If he could come
really within the blazing kernel of darkness, if really he could be
destroyed, burnt away till he lit with her in one consummation, that
were supreme, supreme" (90f.). It would seem to be a pointless
exercise to say that Lawrence used words to represent the wordless.
But there is considerable point in asking why he chose the words he
did. Throughout the novel the spoken world is set over against a
mysterious, inaccessible realm which is essential to the salvation of the
men and women who seek it, or fear it, or forget it. And yet both realms
are "uttered," both exist only as representations in Lawrence's language. Thus the question becomes, what is the status of the very
different languages which Lawrence employs within the novel? Is there
a verbal center to Lawrence's universe, a "unitary" language which is
primary? Or, in choosing to attack the language of instrumental reason
by attempting—impossibly—to stand outside language altogether, has
he given the game away?

Most critics of Lawrence have been well aware of the problems posed by his language, including the difficulties of representing the dark, inarticulate realm which was so important to him. The special language which he employed to evoke that realm is generally distinguished from his more traditional descriptive and narrative techniques. The status of that special language in relation to the other languages within his works is what is at issue. Consider this formulation: "Closely related to this downward search for the first world *n'importe où hors du monde,* is the search for a first language, a purified inward speech as remote from English as the Jurassic is from the modern."[9] To find this "first language" would be to find language as myth—but the difficulty with critical assertions such as this is that they do not always make clear whether they are describing the search for origins as a theme in Lawrence or as a concrete practice which drives his style. The issue is finally one of representation: even as he recounts the failures of his characters' fallen language to reach back to this lost origin, Lawrence names that absence in words. His own writing presumes a transcendent state of being which is revealed in the very failures of language, which he describes as unable to define or exhaust the plenitude it can only suggest.

If this attempt to create a style capable of recovering mythic consciousness is accorded a privileged status in relation to Lawrence's other kinds of language use, the effect of his novels would then be to subordinate history's openness to the categorical demands of an absolute order. For many readers, of course, the linguistic complexities of a character like Birkin have not been particularly problematic, and so the precedence of myth in Lawrence's writings has seemed self-evident. And there is indeed abundant textual evidence to support the picture of Lawrence as priest of a new religion of Being regained. Often the relations between lovers are described in terms which invest very general oppositions such as dark and light with a kind of metaphysical reality: "Sometimes, when his eyes met hers, a yellow flash from them caused a darkness to swoon over her consciousness, electric, and a slight strange laugh came over her face. Her eyes would turn languidly, then close, as if hypnotized. And they lapsed into the same potent darkness" (213). This is Anna with Will, but it might as well have been her mother confronting Tom when he came to ask her to marry him: "She did not know him, only she knew he was a man come for her" (39). Darkness against light, or abstract Male coming to abstract Female, Lawrence's characters lose their particularity at these crucial moments, merging into a universal grammar of identity. When lovers like Anna and Will succeed in evading the everyday, they enter a timeless realm: "As they lay close together, complete and beyond the touch of time and change, it was as if they were at the very centre of all the slow wheeling of space and the rapid agitation of life, deep, deep inside them all, at the centre where there is utter radiance, and eternal being, and the silence absorbed in praise: the steady core of all movements, the unawakened sleep of all wakefulness" (141). In its syntactic repetitions, its diction, and its mystical paradoxes, this language is one with Eliot's "still point of the turning world."

Repeatedly, Lawrence sets this language of timelessness, of an eternal, visionary space, in opposition to the mechanistic world of coal mine and factory. Ursula first makes love with Skrebensky in a setting which is deliberately put into contrast with the machine world below them in the valley, trains climbing and chuffing, furnaces glowing in the night. Unwilling to turn back to that world, the lovers discover a contrary state defined in language that simply blocks out the human time which had produced the coal mines and the railroads: "She passed away as on a dark wind, far, far away, into the pristine darkness of paradise, into the original immortality. She entered the dark fields of immortality" (451). This original paradise is imagined to be regained through a transformation of her very being: "But it was as if she had received another nature. She belonged to the eternal, changeless place into which they had leaped together." This sexual still point is given quite explicitly as an escape from the ugliness and chaos of modern history. In constructing this recurrent discourse of mythic "paradise," Lawrence drew on a number of powerful, related traditions. When Ursula first walks with Skrebensky, for example, she is described as passing under the same ash trees "where her grandfather had walked with his daffodils to make his proposal, and where her mother had gone with her young husband" (298). Even as simple a comparison as this plays its part in assimilating the characters to great organic cycles which are mythic in their transcendence of the more mundane patterns of human endeavor.

In most instances when Lawrence invokes this alternative state of being, he uses language which combines religious and natural imagery. Thus Anna, pregnant, dances naked like David before her unseen Lord, and when she wanders through the flowers in her garden in a kind of trance, the day comes "through the door of Paradise" as a brightness which she then enters, the unborn child shining, and she herself becoming a sunbeam. A particularly striking example of this highly charged, omnivorous style occurs when Will and Anna visit the cathedral. Will's soul "leapt up into the gloom, into possession, it reeled, it swooned with a great escape, it quivered in the womb, in the hush and the gloom of fecundity, like seed of procreation in ecstasy" (198). And Anna joins him, momentarily, in this ecstatic vision: "She too was overcome with wonder and awe. She followed him in his progress. Here, the twilight was the very essence of life, the coloured darkness was the embryo of all light, and the day. Here, the very first dawn was breaking, the very last sunset sinking, and the immemorial darkness, whereof life's day would blossom and fall away again, re-echoed peace and profound immemorial silence" (198). In language such as this, Lawrence is able to equate nature with a metaphysical state which is "always outside of time." By equating embryo and womb with essence, timelessness, and Unity (" 'before' and 'after' were folded together, all was contained in oneness"), Lawrence suppresses the equally plausible (and traditional) use of nature to figure change and difference, the river of time that never flows back, productive of endless variety which, even in a billion oak leaves, never repeats itself. For so many of Lawrence's characters this is indeed the "great escape" from the mechanism and disorder of their age. And however elusive it is for them, it is hardly a state which Lawrence is unable to represent. In a highly metaphoric, incantatory language drawing on religion and nature mysticism, he constructs his myth of origins.

The consequences of such a myth are considerable. Lawrence draws a variety of traditional languages together into a style which is immediately recognizable whenever it appears in his writings. In its figurative repertoire as well as its quasi-biblical rhythms, this style seems to offer itself as a "unitary language," forcing perception into the lines of its absolute thought. Its main thrust is to relegate the public world of work to a subordinate position, while sanctioning personal salvation as the only true hope for any man or woman. Eternal essence takes precedence over the indeterminacy of human history. By constructing this myth which regards salvation as rooted in an organicism which is absolute and eternal, and which explicitly rejects industrial modernity, Lawrence assures his readers that their salvation lies outside history.

However, there is a curious doubleness about that "outside," that saving place which is at the same time always present and always absent. In repeatedly naming his essential, timeless point through organic figures of womb, seed, fecundity, Lawrence suggests that salvation is present only in potential. The individual is shaped only in trivial ways by the prevailing social context because the only shaping that ultimately matters has an inward origin. Like seeds, men and women may be starved or nurtured, but the essential shape of their blossoming cannot be altered by any social ordering. But Lawrence's metaphor is deeply self-contradictory. While salvation is always present in the same way that an oak tree is present in the acorn, it is, for the very reason that it is only potentiality, always absent. As "embryo," the place of salvation is a world which can only be represented, whether hopefully or nostalgically. Lawrence's restless style of continual repetition and change, transforming over and over again the same fundamental paradigms of darkness and light, womb and blossom, One and eternal is itself the sign of a seeking which can never reach its object.

When Lawrence relies on the organic metaphor of human fulfillment as a natural flowering, something apart from the accidents of
history, he supports a discourse which has become increasingly useful
to industry as it moves beyond its nineteenth-century forms. There is
a direct line between Lawrence's myth of organic unfolding and the
more recent proliferation of "human potential" movements. The carefully nurtured social playgrounds surrounding Silicon Valley corpora-
tions, which are in fact as rigidly managed as Gerald Crich's coal
mines, are simply one highly visible sign of an equation which has
proved essential to the more sophisticated stages of industrialization
which have characterized the twentieth century. The structure of work
follows a logic which cannot be questioned because it is "scientific."
But that realm of instrumental necessity has little to do with the true
value and meaning of life, which can only be found through personal
enrichment, or, at its most trivial, "leisure."[10] Thus, in what became
known as "human welfare" and then "liberal management" movements
early in the century, industry learned to encourage a general cultural
tendency to separate work (regarded as a necessary evil) from the
suddenly burgeoning sphere of the Self as an arena where Freudian
psychology and quasi-religious improvement schemes could lead to
unimagined new levels of human fulfillment.[11]

III

The social significance of Lawrence's novels rests primarily with
his language, and particularly with the special language which he
employs in order to represent ecstatic, transitory visions of self-
realization. When Lawrence adopts that special language, he seems to
approach what Bakhtin termed "unitary language," to describe an
absolute, myth-like quality. But for Bakhtin that kind of language has
generally been inimical to the novel. Setting the dialects of a culture
into dialogic play, the novel in his view acts to demystify the very
notion of a unitary language by revealing that all languages are
historically constituted, emerging out of the endless struggles for
self-definition, autonomy, and power which occur within every society.
    Like the host of critics who have explicated Lawrence's "religion of
love," I have quoted passages which illustrate the mythic mode very
nicely. When those passages are examined in a broader context,
however, their unitary force is not so clear. This is Anna in one of those
transcendent moments with Will: "And ever and again he appeared to
her as the dread flame of power. Sometimes, when he stood in the
doorway, his face lit up, he seemed like an annunciation to her, her

heart beat fast. And she watched him, suspended. He had a dark burning being that she dreaded and resisted. She was subject to him as to the Angel of the Presence" (167). This passage is typical of Lawrence's use of biblical language to represent the access of his characters to some higher state of being. And yet a page later, Anna attacks Will for his passionate absorption in the Church: "Did he believe the water turned to wine at Cana? She would drive him to the thing as a historical fact: so much rain-water—look at it—can it become grape-juice, wine? For an instant, he saw with the clear eyes of the mind and said no, his clear mind, answering her for a moment, rejected the idea" (168). The point here is not that two lovers are engaging in a contest of wills over the issue of religious belief. More significant is the fact that two languages, each rooted in long established social practices and institutions, and each capable of organizing experience in distinctly different ways, are being explicitly set into conflict. Just as religious rhythms and imagery bring powerful symbolic associations to the representation of a lover's state, so in Anna's retort there is a complex code of cultural meanings which Will understands perfectly well. Her "look at it" lies in a direct line of descent from Dr. Johnson's famous gesture in which he "refuted" Berkeley by kicking a stone in the road, and it was issuing in Anna's own century in the powerful discourse of middle-class empiricism. For Will the effect of this language of the "clear mind," backed by the Industrial Revolution's quite tangibly productive "reason," is devastating. When he quotes a few more biblical sentences, they ring false to his ear.

When they visit the cathedral, Anna is caught up in Will's enthusiasm, but she finally resists being "cast at last upon the alter steps as upon the shore of the unknown." Her tactic for breaking the power of the myth that threatens to engulf her is simply to focus on the "sly little faces" that are carved in the odd corners of every cathedral: "They knew quite well, these little imps that retorted on man's illusion, that the cathedral was not absolute. They winked and leered, giving suggestion of the many things that had been left out of the great concept of the church. 'However much there is inside here, there's a good deal they haven't got in,' the little faces mocked" (201). Anna is able to evade the church's spell by seeing its "great concept" as necessarily partial, an impressive figure to be sure, but one which has been drawn against a ground that constitutes its opposite. Those imps speak a language of parody which cannot but destroy the cathedral's grand spell, and they are always present to any eye that would raise them out of their usual invisibility. Anna goes on from her discovery to play a kind of rabbit/duck game of perception with Will in which she sees a stone figure as female while he sees a clean-shaven monk. Will is once again furious to have his "vital illusions" mocked, but his response is finally more complex. With a part of himself he responds

more deeply to the impish faces than he had before to the grandeur of
the cathedral. In this reversal of pattern he not only sees his cathedrals
as no longer absolute, but he learns to see them as "a world within a
world," rather than as a world within a chaos. That is, they constitute
one pattern among many, not, as he had previously believed, an
absolute order beyond which was only meaningless confusion.

For all his yearning for myth-like certainty, Lawrence in *The
Rainbow* actually seems to delight in overturning what had seemed to
be stable and coherent figures. Impish faces appear everywhere. Anna
sits in church and subjects sacred language to the corrosive action of
bourgeois practicality: "Was this what she had come to hear: how by
doing this thing and not by doing that, she could save her soul?" (154).
In the next generation, Ursula deconstructs the low church myth of
Christ's common humanity: "What would Jesus do, if he were in my
shoes?" (273). And Tom Brangwen, whose love for Lydia had been
described as a "baptism to another life," makes a speech at Anna's
wedding which reduces such language to utter emptiness: " 'If we've
got to be Angels,' went on Tom Brangwen, haranguing the company at
large, 'and if there is no such thing as a man nor a woman amongst
them, then it seems to me as a married couple makes one Angel.' 'It's
the brandy,' said Alfred Brangwen wearily" (134). Still another counterpoint is sounded when Ursula learns to speak the rationalizing
language of Winifred Inger's "scientific education": "Christianity accepted crucifixion to escape from fear: 'Do your worst to me, that I may
have no more fear of the worst' " (340).

As might be expected, the mutual unweaving of one language by
another is even more marked in *Women in Love*. Consider the medley
of codes which constitute this characteristic exchange between Birkin
and Ursula. Birkin calls on the mythic language of timelessness:
" 'What I want is a strange conjunction with you'—he said quietly;
'—not meeting and mingling;—you are quite right:—but an equilib-
rium, a pure balance of two single beings:—as the stars balance each
other.' " Ursula's reply employs the witty social dialogue of a Noel
Coward play: " 'Isn't this rather sudden?' she mocked." And Birkin
returns in an ironic quotation of the language of the "real world":
" 'Best to read the terms of the contract, before we sign,' he said" (139).

Examples such as these can be found in every chapter of *The
Rainbow* and *Women in Love*, and their presence does not simply mean
that Lawrence had a good ear for the rich variety of speech in his
world. Lawrence was hardly a naive realist, and the world he created
in these novels was anything but a seamless linguistic whole. In
continually showing the languages that make up his text to be
historically constituted and partial, Lawrence refused to allow even his
evocation of a myth-like salvation to gain unquestioned hegemony

over the alternative codes of industrial managers, avant-garde intellectuals, inarticulate farmers, bohemian artists, and bourgeois moralists.

It might be argued that Lawrence's refusal to validate fully even his visionary speech is (like Birkin's letter becoming self-parody when read to cafe intellectuals) simply the sign of language's inadequacy to recapture its transcendent object. But the linguistic discontinuities which fissure these texts so deeply might better be read for what they reveal about the constitution of the human subject. It is important to recognize, first of all, that the distinct social dialects which Lawrence employs so richly are not only spoken by distinct individuals. Each of the major characters in these novels could be shown to speak (or to be represented by) a great variety of different and often contradictory languages. Just as there is no unitary language, there are no characters who are perfectly self-identical.

In attempting to understand how Lawrence's characters assume their identities, it is essential to remember that they do so first of all in language:

> "Why, what ca' it then?" "It's hair." "Hair! Wheriver dun they rear that sort?" "Wheriver dun they?" she asked, in dialect, her curiosity overcoming her.
>
> Instead of answering he shouted with joy. It was the triumph, to make her speak dialect. (84)

If this meeting of two dialects seems little more than a trivial game, played by young Anna and the townspeople, Lawrence immediately reminds us, through her father, that it is not. Brangwen's response to this interlude is to suddenly feel the cultural difference which this linguistic gap reveals—and sustains. He discovers a secret desire to make Anna a lady, and he thinks about his brother's mistress, who is indeed of a higher class. Lawrence then describes Brangwen's visit to this lady, an experience which makes him acutely aware of how different a life can be from his own, and which causes him to despise himself, momentarily, as a boor and a clodhopper. The simple narrative sequence which Lawrence initiates in this scene represents a perception of the vital link between language and history which reappears in many ways throughout the novels.

The gross linguistic difference of class dialect is only one of the forms which this link assumes. When Ursula is growing out of childhood, for instance, she finds the literary conventions of romance and learns to identify with an image of womanhood inseparable from its archaically poetic diction ("whilst she, ah, she, would remain the lonely maid high up and isolated in the tower"). Language such as this plays its part in the complex social determination of sexual identity, and Lawrence is explicit in showing Ursula's passage through a series of distinct social discourses, each contributing to her character. This is one of her languages when she has become a young woman: "It is your child, and for that reason I must revere it and submit my body entirely to its welfare, entertaining no thought of death, which once more is largely conceit. Therefore, because you once loved me, and because this child is your child, I ask you to have me back. If you will cable me one word, I will come to you as soon as I can. I swear to you to be a dutiful wife, and to serve you in all things" (484). The vulnerable maid in the tower is still present here, though submerged now in the more recent discourse of the subservient bourgeois wife.

Lawrence's immediate comment on her letter to Skrebensky is especially interesting in its conjoining of writing and the self: "This letter she wrote, sentence by sentence, as if from her deepest, sincerest heart. She felt that now, now, she was at the depths of herself. This was her true self, forever. With this document she would appear before God at the Judgment Day." Lawrence's "as if" stands out as the marker for an irony which pervades this passage, and which would undermine the absolute, religious moment of access to the "deepest self" even without the dramatic irony of Skrebensky's marriage. There is no eternal center of the self which can be inscribed in a "document" and presented to God as a kind of personal Logos. On the other hand, the self which Ursula displays in her letter is no illusion. If Lawrence parodies a language compacted of biblical imagery, sentimental romance, and middle-class sexual stereotyping, he also shows Ursula to be struggling with this complex identity, both in this novel and in *Women in Love*. She does indeed write herself down, sentence by sentence, but the words have all been said before. Like some unconscious plagiarist, she simply writes—and feels—a language which is so pervasive in her culture that it seems to be her own.

The volatility of character in Lawrence has been a key issue for his critics, who often seem to share more assumptions in this area than in most others. A socially oriented critic, for example, can write that *The Rainbow* "provides little of the data necessary for interpreting the feelings and actions of characters in terms of their social situation. The 'natural' conflict, the organic disturbance between men and women in the novel, appears to be rooted so deep in individual character, to be so much a matter of the impersonal unconscious, as to escape social determination."[12] And for a critic whose general interest is more psychological, Lawrence's representation of human identity is seen as equally divorced from "social determination." Despairing of the possibility of historical reconstruction, Lawrence is said to turn instead to an individuality which is assumed to exist prior to the social constitution of the self: "Personal relations become increasingly difficult as society loses the confidence to tell us what these relations ought to be. As a result we start from scratch. Each individual retreats into his own shell, and every relation becomes a power struggle modified only by our need to rub up against each other for mutual pleasure or advantage."[13] Or consider this particularly economical statement: "D. H. Lawrence's main concern is identity, and the fragmented self. It is not 'blood' religion, nor modern sexuality, nor the vicissitudes of the industrial age."[14]

Although there are clearly many ways to dismiss social history as merely a series of uninteresting "vicissitudes," what remains of the self after society is removed from the equation is not so simple a question. Whether the metaphor be "deeply rooted" character, or a "shell" into which one may retreat, there is an assumption that identity has an essential and permanent being which is apart from whatever historical accidents it may encounter. Frederic Jameson has placed this "fiction of the individual subject" in a larger context of social readjustment which was occurring throughout the nineteenth century. Viewing "so-called bourgeois individualism" as a necessary element in the ideology of the free market economy, and so as acting to sustain the power of the class which had created that economy, he argues that as the notion of the autonomous individual became more difficult to support, in the face of modern disintegration and powerlessness, increasingly desperate strategies were employed to assure its continuing viability.[15]

For Jameson, the best literary enactment of the new myth of individual autonomy lies in Henry James's innovation in point of view, "which comes into being as a protest and a defense against reification, [and] ends up furnishing a powerful ideological instrument in the perpetuation of an increasingly subjectivized and psychologized world. . . ." But James's interiorization of consciousness should be contrasted with Lawrence's careful delineation of the historical grounding of his characters' identities, in languages like those which shape the young Ursula. Given the overwhelming tendency of critics to regard Lawrence's characters as struggling toward identities which are touched only incidentally by the details of historical context, the success of his effort to bring this historical grounding to consciousness is questionable. But the multiple discourses which Lawrence depicts are real, and historically specific, and he explicitly shows how those social languages are appropriated by men and women—in their letters, their conversations with each other, and in their own self-understandings.

It is characteristic of Lawrence to present the delineation of the self as struggle and contradiction. His characters often speak about their true, deep selves, and yet that talk mostly functions as resistance to the social codes which are in fact shaping their words, their actions, even their feelings. By invoking a counter possibility of absolute selfhood, even as an empty category, Lawrence's men and women call into question the inevitability, the "naturalness" of the social languages which they must speak even as they learn to resist. The public world is always present to Lawrence's characters, revealing itself in moments as private as Ursula's ecstasy of dutiful submissiveness. But from the first page of *The Rainbow* that public world is figured most sharply by the new industrial landscape that shadows the consciousness of all the characters. As many critics have pointed out, Tom Brangwen is a precursor of Gerald Crich, and though he remains in the background through most of *The Rainbow,* he is, like Gerald, a presence which cannot be escaped. Arguing with Ursula about the condition of the miners, he offers the novel's bluntest description of the social determination of the human subject: "They believe they must alter themselves to fit the pits and the place, rather than alter the pits and the place to fit themselves. It is easier" (346). The most interesting part of this statement is its "they believe," which raises the central issue of the dialogue which follows.

Tom, Ursula, and Winifred all deplore the exploitation of the miners quite explicitly, and yet all are finally implicated in the structure of power which supports that exploitation. Ursula's condemnation is violent, and she understands well enough that the power of social structures exists only insofar as it is reproduced in the knowledge and the actions of individuals: "It had only to be forsaken to be inane, meaningless" (349). But in formulating her insight she unwittingly supports the very discourse she would destroy: "Let them starve and grub in the earth for roots, rather than serve such a Moloch as this." The mines do not in fact disappear when Ursula shuts her eyes because they are sustained by a language empowered by its very difference from the archaism of mythic preaching. This is Tom, the mine manager, agreeing with Ursula about the poor conditions in the pits: "Yes, they are pretty bad. The pits are very deep, and hot, and in some places wet. The men die of consumption fairly often. But they earn good wages" (347). This is the discourse of expedient rationality, of cost-benefit analysis, and it accounts for the men's belief that they must alter themselves to serve the pits because it is a discourse which has assumed the invisibility of "natural law." For Tom, it permits an easy movement from describing the men as artificially shaped to their work to the subsequent acceptance of that shape as quite natural: "But that's how they are."

Almost everything Lawrence wrote might be seen as a struggle to evade the power of Tom's simple assertion. In representing the rich and contradictory languages through which men and women receive their identities, he depicted both the substance for Tom's confident sense of a stable self, and the simultaneous excess which can reveal that stability to be merely arbitrary and provisional. Ursula's words, or Birkin's, or Tom Brangwen's all may be seen to play a part in the complex discursive economy of the age which so troubles them. They all contribute to a closure which makes history seem to be inevitable, unquestionable. But in the counterpoint of their various languages, in the interweaving of Genesis and Bentham, regional dialect and lady-talk, bourgeois maxim and sentimental romance, Lawrence opens the self, and history, to human making. He is with the other modernists in this use of textual discontinuity to break the illusory wholeness of the constituted subject. But like them, he may be read very differently, his writings searched out for a single voice, the gaps that constitute linguistic difference suppressed, a "vision" defined. In preserving certain basic assumptions of English culture with regard to the properly hierarchical relation between work and practical knowledge, and the "higher" realm of morality and self-realization, Lawrence's texts display a congruence with the dominant discourse of instrumental reason which tends to deflect the power of his social critique. Nevertheless, the linguistic discontinuities of his writing do stand against the powerful knowledge of his age, and his texts can undermine that knowledge if they are read, in light of their social origins, as the dialogic pattern of a history which is always closing but never closed.

Chapter 5

History as Language: William Carlos Williams

I

William Carlos Williams was no less interested in the condition of work in the twentieth century than was his friend Ezra Pound. But Williams had little time in his busy medical practice for the kind of extensive (though sometimes quirky) reading in which Pound could indulge. While he was familiar with Pound's most "essential" authors—C. H. Douglas and Brooks Adams, for example—Williams's reading did not extend to more specialized discussions, such as that of Dexter Kimball, on the possibility of humanizing scientific management. But if Williams was less well read than Pound in the documents of modern industrialization, he was far more familiar with the actual working lives of men and women than either Pound or the Lawrence whose avant-garde associations had carried him far from his childhood roots in England's industrial midlands. Treating patients who, in the early years, came primarily from the working classes, and later dealing with a more middle-class clientele he described as "commuters,"[1] Williams defined another dimension of modernism's engagement with the world of work. His writings deal with a wide range of specific work experience, but beyond that level of concrete depiction they also attempt to diagnose the larger social and economic transformations which were altering the lives of individual men and women. His diagnosis may have been intuitive, and his prescription a kind of folk cure, and, like Lawrence, his language

93

sometimes unwittingly reproduced important assumptions of the very modernity with which he was contending. Nevertheless, Williams succeeded as well as any of his contemporaries in defining the dangers of an instrumental reason which had become fundamental to the new order of industrial society.

The potential of many different kinds of work to offer the satisfaction of fine craftsmanship had always appealed to Williams. In "Fine Work with Pitch and Copper," for example, he observes a roofer:

> The copper in eight
> foot strips has been
> beaten lengthwise
>
> down the center at right
> angles and lies ready
> to edge the coping
>
> One still chewing
> picks up a copper strip
>
> and runs his eye along it[2]

Like W. H. Hudson's shepherd or Pound's Renaissance stonemason, this roofer is practicing a pre-industrial trade, but the image of workers such as these exercising genuine control over their tasks is invariably an important element in any attempt to portray the degradation of work within advanced industrial societies.

In his series of novels based on the lives of his wife's parents, Williams depicts his hero Joe Stecher's working life as largely a struggle to retain some pride in his craft of printing against the opposition of both management and a corrupt union movement. In *In the Money*, Stecher meets the president of the United States, and afterward bemoans the consequences of increasingly centralized planning, in this instance in the form of government "policy": "You stop paying attention to the truth of the detail. You don't look to see whether that man is an honest man, whether he's doing the job well or ill. All you care about is, My policy." Stecher's self-identity as an old-world master printer depends on the association of work and morality. Work is by no means simply the expedient means to an end such as profit: "They don't know what excellence means. No, not one of them. They simply don't know that it means to do one thing well. The rest—? To do it well. Honestly. Every day. And never to lie. Never."[3]

Against the increasing remoteness of bureaucratic planning, Williams sets the immediacy of union violence, including industrial sabotage, which had been one of the initial problems which Frederick Taylor had set out to overcome before the turn of the century. In *White Mule*, the first of the Stecher trilogy, Williams describes an incident in which a printing press is jammed after a screwdriver is intentionally dropped into it during a period of labor-management hostility.[4] In that novel, Stecher is depicted as standing between an exploitative management and a union which he regards as corrupt, and which threatens him with physical violence during a strike. Throughout Williams's writings, the industrial workplace is characterized by a latent violence which always threatens to emerge in one form or another. In a short story such as "The Paid Nurse," for example, a worker is burned in a chemical explosion, only to be forced to return to work immediately upon the threat of losing his job. He is forbidden to see anyone other than the company doctor, whose job it is to keep him working and to avoid paying any compensation claim—not to sympathize with his pain, or even to offer proper medical care.[5] Even when working men and women appear in the poems and stories without explicit mention of their work, as in the many accounts of doctor-patient encounters, the presence of the industrial world from which these characters come is implied, in their economic need, their social cynicism, and the physical hurt which often brings them to the narrator's attention.

Williams did not make the mistake, however, of imagining that industrialization in the twentieth century was still primarily a matter of physical oppression, like that in a nineteenth-century thread mill. The physical violence was there, of course, but the process of industrial rationalization had come to govern millions of lives beyond the factory gates as well: "As rabbits are cottontailed the office-workers in cotton running pants get in a hot car, ride in a hot tunnel and confine themselves in a hot office—to sell asphalt, the trade in tanned leather. The trade in everything. Things they've never seen, will never own and can never name. Not even an analogous name do they know. As a carter, knowing the parts of a wagon will know, know, touch, the parts of—a woman."[6] The carter is like the roofer in knowing his work as whole and immediate, and he too serves as a foil against the remoteness, the abstraction of the work performed in Manhattan offices.

In a speech on the subject of social credit which he delivered a few years after his 1928 description of the rabbit-like office workers, Williams asserted that the present age may be distinguished from the one preceding it by the increasing subordination of actual workers within the processes of production: "This is the Power Age as contrasted with an age just preceding it when Labor was predominant. This is an age in which the productive capacity of one man has been increased, by machines, forty times over former standards, but during which purchasing power, as represented by wages or their equivalent, though it should have been expanded forty times to meet this contingency, has remained relatively stationary."[7] It was at this level of the newly systematic organization of production that the diminished autonomy, and consequently the diminished self-identity, of workers was based. As early as 1909, Williams had observed the systematizing of work in Germany (which, as described in Chapter 1, was a concern of both Pound and Ford, who understood its implications for the rest of the industrialized world). Writing to his brother from Leipzig, he complained that "the whole life here is a picture of economy, specialization, long hard systematized work and a quiet perseverance. I do not admire the types I have seen so far and I do not think the people as a nation are gifted with inspiration."[8]

In 1909, Williams did not yet fully understand the significance of the systematizing of work which he observed, ascribing it too simply to the national character of the Germans. By 1940, when he published the second volume of his Stecher trilogy, however, Williams had come to see the economic realm in much more historical terms, as a contested field shaped by competing ideologies and individual wills rather than by racial identities. He makes the force of ideology clear by having Stecher debate a business associate with reference to the question of allowing a closed shop: " 'That's their business.' 'Oh no it isn't, Stecher. That's where you're wrong. A thousand conflicting factors operate that none of us understands as yet. That's where the trouble's going to come from.' The men sat quiet again looking out into the slushy street. 'It's all right to talk about paying a living wage, but in business those things are beyond the control of the individual—and he's got to make up his mind' " (IM, 292). Like the apologists for scientific management whom I discussed in Chapter 2, this businessman is invoking the powerful discourse of economic law: "Maybe I'm wrong. Maybe everything's wrong, the whole business and economic setup. But we've got to live with it and make it serve us today or it'll finish us." Though Williams's version of the discourse is self-deprecating and disarming to a degree, its import is unambiguous: inevitable economic forces shape the relations of production, not human effort or intention.

In addition to the assumption that something like inevitable economic law does exist, this passage employs a related discourse of expediency which Williams understood to be a crucial part of the ideology of the new industrial order. In his prologue to "Kora in Hell," he had spoken of "a science doing slavery service upon gas engines,"[9] that is, of the appropriation of science to serve the ends of industry. This union of science and business did not characterize the earlier stages of the industrial revolution, but it was a fundamental premise of later developments such as scientific management. Williams's hostility to the direction which science had taken reached its fullest expression in his philosophical musings of 1928–30, *The Embodiment of Knowledge*, where he argued that "at the beginning of the century a child could see that as a major occupation of the intelligence science was finished. At such a time multiplication of services takes the place of serious effort, and the type of genius represented by Thomas Edison is predominant, the theories of 'service' (not the fact), the pragmatism, and philosophical (cinematizations) (slow motion) amateurs were turned up."[10]

Pound had also used Edison as his symbol of a new and destructive kind of social logic when he wrote (also in 1928) that he would not allow his right foot to be cut off just to make room in the bottom of automobiles. And for Williams, too, it was not the inventions—the light bulbs and phonographs—to which he objected, but the logic which accorded them an increasingly honored place in the national scheme of values. It was a question of the way in which knowledge itself had come to be used:

> Machinery as an effect of complicated knowledge has many aspects to the individual—some of which show it to be out of hand. That is, there are aspects to machinery quite apart from the technical ones involved in its mechanical conception, practicalization and operation. It is mystery just as patent as the virgin birth until it be solved and man replaced in knowledge above it. As soon as we make it we must at once plan to escape—and escape. (EK, 62)

In his demand that quasireligious attitudes toward the machine must be demystified, Williams anticipated Lewis Mumford, who would argue just a few years later that "only as a religion can one explain the compulsive nature of the urge toward mechanical development without regard for the actual outcome of the development in human relations themselves."[11] And like recent scholars who have argued against technological determinism,[12] Williams understood that subjection to the machine depended upon our perceiving knowledge itself as somehow autonomous, as no longer within our control. This is how he defines the "escape" he proposes:

> By this we understand the escape of man from domination by his own engines. Thus continually he asserts himself above what he knows and which has tended to fix him as part of itself. To stop before any machine is to make of it a fetish attended by its metaphysical priest the engineer. It is not necessarily to be an engineer to conceive the place of a machine, nor is it easy to escape them. On the contrary the knowledge of an engineer, being so in particular, is likely to absorb him into itself until he becomes a scientist—limited, segregated— unable to escape. (EK, 62f.)

For Williams, as for Pound, this instrumental reason which teaches us to worship the machine must be confronted in society's educational institutions. He had very little but criticism for the practices of the "cultural departments" which "continued to mull over the old records, gallivanting back and forth upon the trodden-out tracks of past initiative, in a daze of subserviency and impotence" (SE, 159). He saw economics behind the bending of society's official institutions for the production of new thought to the task of perpetuating the status quo: "Subserviency is the correct term; for the power of wealth, which by endowments makes the university and its faculty possible, at the same time keeps that power, by control of salaries and trustees' votes, in order to dictate what those who teach must and must not say. And the teachers submit to it." In *The Embodiment of Knowledge*, he argues that "it is not the purpose of colleges just to teach the steps to a 'profession,' to make itself into a mechanical master to apprentices in rather cultured trades" (EK, 4). Specifically, he criticizes the "synthetic method," which he characterizes as "squeezing the matters for study up into small parcels, by simplification, by getting to the 'essentials' in each subject" (EK, 4). Williams goes on to include the "official magazines" in his account of society's mechanisms of self-replication, and with Pound he argues that the publishing industry has come to be ruled by an economic expediency, in which authors have felt their own autonomy slipping away in the face of inexorable pressures to produce literary products suitable for the marketplace. As writers are forced to "create by code" to specifications determined elsewhere in a hierarchy of business and government, they too must feel the distortions which a society ruled by instrumental reason imposes upon all work (RI, 108). Art, advertising, and the elementary school reading text, with its thirty-five-word vocabulary, all coalesce:

> —and we have
> :the script writer advising
> "every line to be like
> a ten word telegram" but
> neglecting to add, "to a
> child of twelve"—obscene
> beyond belief.[13]

II

That Williams promoted the "local" from every available soapbox is well known. But the notion of localism was more than simply a guide to poetic content. One of the premises on which he based his critique of instrumental reason was that such a pattern of thought was historically contingent, and so could only be opposed on the historically specific ground which had brought it into being. In his essay, "The American Background," he criticizes Emerson as a writer who could have been truly great had he not attempted to create a fabric of thought independent of the historical condition of America in the early nineteenth century: "The wrenchings of fate at his elbow, occupation with which would have put him beside the older efforts on a first-rate, if cruder, basis, he avoided or missed by rising superior to them into a world of thought which he believed to be universal only because he couldn't see whence it had arisen. It had a ground, all must, but it was not his, while his remained neglected" (SE, 155). What is important about a statement such as this is not its repetition of the old argument about how art in America should break free of its European tradition, but rather the insistence that all thought is grounded in a time and a place, that Emerson's supposed universality is really an evasion of the historical struggles of his own age.

One of the consequences of this belief in the historicity of thought is its corollary that all statements are potentially implicated in the political contentions of their time. Thus language is regarded by Williams as available to whatever interests are strong enough to appropriate it, and in an age dominated by the instrumental reason of advanced capitalism, language will most likely serve to reinforce an ethos of profitable expediency. In "The Simplicity of Disorder," he denounces a condition in which "language is subservient to the sale of old clothes and ideas and the formulas for the synthetic manufacture of rubber" (SE, 96). And he accuses those who should oppose such a condition:

> Did the academicians but know it, it is the surrealists who have invented the living defense of literature, that will supplant science; and it is they who betray their trust by allowing the language to be enslaved by its enemies; the philosophers and the venders of manure and all who cry their wares in the street and put up signs: 'House for sale.'
>
> Language, which is the hope of man, is by this enslaved, forced, raped, made a whore by the idea venders.

In his *Autobiography*, Williams offers an account of the way in which he imagines language becoming subject to the social formulas of a commodified world. He describes his experience as a physician able to witness what he calls "the words being born" in all their "unspoiled newness."[14] As the babies he delivers grow up, however, they are trapped by the "lying dialectics" of society's institutions. By dialectics, he means "any arbitrary system, which, since all systems are mere inventions, is necessarily in each case a false premise, upon which a closed system is built shutting those who confine themselves to it from the rest of the world." The notion that the men and women he treats have been constrained by closed and arbitrary systems was very important to Williams. Now, we might say that what he was describing was his society's hegemonic discourse, in order to point out that Williams was positing a process which takes place within language, and which results in limiting social relations to patterns which serve the ends of dominant groups or institutions.

A term such as "hegemony" would have been useful to Williams in constructing his argument about the "lying dialectics" which imprison his patients because it implies the domination of a field rather than its absolute transformation into an order which excludes all counter possibilities. Thus Williams begins his argument by referring to those aspects of his patients' lives which elude the forms of knowing which they have been taught: "What was that? We can't name it; we know it never gets into any recognizable avenue of expression" (A, 360). And this is precisely why the installation of a detailed program such as scientific management, as well as the opposition to its underlying rhetoric of instrumental reason, depends on the mastery of social discourse. For Williams, if we cannot name it, it can neither be represented nor can it shape human consciousness.

Williams's clearest statement of this process, and its social consequences, is perhaps his poem, "The Forgotten City." In the poem, he describes a drive back to the city with his mother during a hurricane. The storm forces him off the familiar parkways into neighborhoods which he had never seen before. The storm is described as having broken

> the barrier and let through
> a strange commonplace: Long, deserted avenues
> with unrecognized names at the corners and
> drunken looking people with completely
> foreign manners.
>
> (CLP, 49)

This is a world that is both strange and yet commonplace—that is, it has been there all along, though unknown to the poet. The poem assumes the voice of an anthropologist, noting the habits of an unknown tribe, but the mockery is directed at the poet's own ignorance:

> I had no idea where I was and promised myself
> I would some day go back to study this
> curious and industrious people who lived
> in these apartments, at these sharp
> corners and turns of intersecting avenues
> with so little apparent communication
> with an outside world. How did they get
> cut off this way from representation in our
> newspapers and other means of publicity
> when so near the metropolis, so closely
> surrounded by the familiar and the famous?

To be cut off from representation is to have fallen outside of the limited set of discursive patterns which society seeks to reproduce. It is to exist, if at all, only as powerless Other to the dominant culture.

Williams was always interested in the forms of representation within his society, and particularly in the way those forms were constrained through the institutional practices of universities, newspapers, and publishing houses. In his efforts to trace the suffering of the working men and women depicted in his stories and poems to systematic features of the modern economic order, his examination of the ideological weight of social discourse was more fully thought through, and more original, than his rather half-hearted borrowings of social credit theory from Pound. In a poem such as "A Woman in Front of a Bank," for example, Williams anticipates the study of semiotics by pointing out the socially significant iconology of bank architecture:

> The bank is a matter of columns,
> like   .   convention,
> unlike invention; but the pediments
> sit there in the sun
>
> to convince the doubting of
> investments "solid
> as rock"—upon which the world
> stands, the world of finance,
>
> the only world . . .
>   (CLP 70)

If the bank represents "convention," the contrasting notion of "invention"—or that vitality which exceeds the constraints which convention would impose—is given in the image of a woman in a pink cotton dress, standing in front of the bank, rocking a baby carriage.

The bank's facade speaks a message of authority grounded in the absolute objectivity of laws of finance. But language is a primary site of this struggle between invention and the various closures which would fix men and women in familiar patterns. Prior to *Paterson*, Williams's most ambitious attempts to explore the nature of socially constraining discourse took place in prose works, particularly *The Great American Novel* and *In the American Grain*. The heroine of *The Great American Novel* is a little Ford car, which (who?) at one point dreams about being a woman: "The little car purred pleasantly to itself at the thought of the long night. Oh, to be a woman, thought the speeding mechanism. For they had wrapped something or other in a piece of newspaper and placed it under the seat and there were pictures there of girls—or grown women it might be, in very short skirts" (I, 190). The point of Williams's irony, of course, is that it is not automobiles, but men and women who are "mechanisms," and whose self-identities, like that of the Ford car, are constructed by the language of newspapers.

The passage continues in a parody of advertising style: "The perfection of Pisek-designed Personality Modes: A distinctly forward move in the realm of fashion is suggested by the new personality modes, designed by Pisek . . . modes that are genuine inspirations of individual styling, created for meeting the personal preferences of a fastidiously fashionable clientele, the woman and the miss who seek personality in dress in keeping with their charms, characteristics and station" (I, 190f.). This familiar public language seeks to constitute the woman as sexual object, while at the same time offering her a position of dominance within the hierarchy of social power—her clothes, like the pillars of the bank, will bespeak her proper "station."

Williams does not simply describe these various social languages, but reproduces them in the kind of ventriloquism which Bakhtin ascribes to the novel. He lets us hear dialects which are determined not by ethnic origin or geographical region, but by the rules of an increasingly subdivided and specialized economic discourse. And more important, by placing them into ironic conjunctions, he reminds us that these voices have been artificially imitated. At one point in *The Great American Novel*, we hear a fragment of ordinary conversation: "You know last Sunday was my birthday. Seventy-three years old. I had a party—my relatives came from all sides. But I couldn't get her downstairs. She's afraid. We had a banister put on the stairs, cost me nine dollars but she will not do it. She's so fat you know, she's afraid of falling" (I, 203). The effect of the human detail of this passage is to make clear that the discursive principle of the paragraph which follows is to remove all sign of the human voice, and to suggest instead that some kind of inscrutable economic law is speaking: "Re Commissions due—Amount $1.00. Dear Sir:—You will please take notice that unless we receive payment in full of your account within FIVE DAYS after receipt of this letter, we shall draw upon you for the amount due" (I, 203). Williams's parody of the authorless solemnity of this kind of writing was part of an important series of experiments in which style was forced to call attention to itself as arbitrary form, rather than simply passing before us in its usual transparent familiarity.

The most complex representation of a powerful social language occurs at the end of *The Great American Novel*, when the narrator visits a factory which makes thermometers. Responding to an implied question about industrial accidents, specifically the danger of mercury poisoning, a manager of some sort replies in a voice which combines the folksiness of the man with the fat wife with a discourse of benevolently regulated technological expertise: "The glass blowers have never in my entire experience of 17 years suffered any harm from their trade. Why we had a boy in the old factory, a cripple, a withered leg, the weakest, scrawniest lad you ever saw. He's been blowing for us for 15 or 17 years and you should see him today. Why the fat fairly hangs down over his collar" (I, 225). The fatherly tone of this passage is then supported by a technical explanation of the factory's procedures ("volatilization," "capillary tube," etc.), creating a rhetorical effect of old-fashioned good will informed by a scientific assurance which only experts would dare to question. Of course, Williams does not leave the reader without a suggestion about how such rhetoric should be read: "Sometimes, of course, a bulb breaks in heating so that the floor is full of the stuff."

III

In the American Grain was a more serious book than *The Great American Novel,* and it carried the orchestration of multiple discourses to much greater lengths. But in its treatment of historical materials, it raises new questions of interpretation. When Williams set out to write his own history of America, he was using the historical materials in two distinct ways. First of all, when he wrote about Cotton Mather or Daniel Boone, he was always in fact writing about the present, about life in the America of the 1920s. In his *Autobiography,* he says that he wanted "to give the impression, an inclusive definition, of what these men of whom I am writing have come to be for us. That they have made themselves part of us and that that is what we are. I want to make it clear that they are us, the American make-up, that we are what they have made us by their deeds" (A, 236). This is in part a rhetorical strategy, and a familiar one at that. I have already discussed, for example, Henri Le Chatelier's preface to the French edition of Taylor's *Principles of Scientific Management,* in which history, from the French Revolution to the present, is employed to define the supposed needs of the present and to argue against objections to Taylor's program. Similarly, when Williams berates the Puritans so heatedly, his argument is clearly directed against his own contemporaries, because "they are us."

But they are also said to have made us what we are, a statement which assumes historical causality. If the first use of history is primarily rhetorical, Williams nevertheless also sought genuine historical explanation. He believed that the condition of work in the twentieth century had its roots in the institutional struggles as well as the metaphysical attitudes of the early years of the American settlements. Alexander Hamilton was the key figure in his historical analysis, and in a 1936 speech, he succinctly defined his thesis: "The democratic principle in economic affairs fought hard to preserve itself useful and intact but succumbed in the end to Hamilton's successful drive for an industrial autocracy and consequent economic centralization under narrow control. From that time on economic freedom of the individual was a lost cause" (RI, 101). The principal fact here, as Williams saw it, was a commitment on the part of the new nation to centralized control within industry, with a consequent erosion of the individual's autonomy.

The Hamilton of *In the American Grain* is important primarily for his economic schemes. Williams characterizes Hamilton's achievement by responding to the tag, "protector of liberty":

> Whose, Hamilton's?—to harness the whole, young aspiring genius to a treadmill? Paterson he wished to make capital of the country because there was waterpower there which to his time and mind seemed colossal. And so he organized a company to hold the land thereabouts, with dams and sluices, the origin today of the vilest swillhole in christendom, the Passaic River; impossible to remove the nuisance so tight had he, Hamilton, sewed up his privileges unto kingdomcome, through his holding company, in the State legislature. *His* company. *His* United States: Hamiltonia—the land of the company.[15]

In Williams's eyes, the aim of Hamilton's program was to channel the natural vitality of the new land into his water mill, just as he would trap ordinary Americans into the treadmill of a newly industrializing nation.

Hamilton's nemesis was Aaron Burr, and Burr allows Williams to articulate a counter view. Burr "saw America, or he had seen America, as a promise of delight and it struck fine earth, that fancy. Now he saw a sombre Washington—with shrewd dog Hamilton at his side—locking the doors, closing the windows, building fences and providing walls. He dreaded this. He saw that they would only lock up themselves, and he rebelled" (IAG, 187). The idea of closing off, locking up, appears again and again in *In the American Grain,* and it is central to Williams's analysis of that potentiality in American history which succeeded in becoming dominant and which ultimately led to the blighted industrial landscape of so much of his own writing. Figures like Benjamin Franklin are seen to be building up, penny by penny, "a fort to be secure in" (IAG, 156). Afraid of the unruly vitality of the New World, Franklin constructs his ideology of thrift as a way of controlling uncertainty.

The chapter about Burr and Hamilton is entitled "The Virtue of History," and before he begins to discuss their lives, Williams makes clear why history itself is important and what it has to do with closing and locking: "That of the dead which exists in our imaginations has as much fact as have we ourselves. The premise that serves to fix us fixes also that part of them which we remember" (IAG, 189). Like history writing, we are also shaped and limited by "premises," which is to say, by the discourse we have been taught. In the case of Burr and Hamilton, the dominant premise, which Williams would challenge, is that Hamilton was the nation's benefactor, while Burr was a dangerous and unpredictable rebel. But since Williams sees "history," and the reader of history, as having both been shaped by the same premises, the present may, in his view, be controlled by a past which is no more than a text—the story of a hero, Hamilton, for example, rather than the story of greed and oppression.

Thus when Williams attempts to trace his present in America's past, he creates a kind of Manichean fiction in which two principles compete. Hamilton, with his treadmills and dams, and Franklin, with his thrifty fort, are part of a pattern which began with "murder and enslavement" (IAG, 39), as the first explorers slaughtered the Indians and exploited the land, but which "might have begun differently." The Puritans define one extreme in this part of the story for Williams. The separation into clear, discrete human categories, which was crucial to Hamilton's scheme for economic power, had its origin in the world of the Puritans: "Lost, in this (and its environments) as in a forest, I do believe the average American to be an Indian, but an Indian robbed of his world—unless we call machines a forest in themselves" (IAG, 128). This is the condition of men and women in the present, isolated and alienated among their machines, but Williams is less interested in the machines themselves—so often and so simply blamed for this alienation—than he is in the gradual reshaping of the self: "Steadily the individual loses caste, then the local government loses its author- ity; the head is more removed. Finally the center is reached—totally dehumanized, like a Protestant heaven. Everything is Federalized and all laws become prohibitive in essence." The crucial movement here is the draining away of the individual's power and knowledge to an increasingly remote center from which all law originates. Always absent, that center is nevertheless the enabling premise of the Puritan world: "They pleaded weakness, they called continually for help (while working shrewdly with their own hands all the while), they asked protection—but the real help had been to make them small, small and several, several and each as a shell for his own 'soul.' And the soul? a memory (or a promise), a flower sheared away—nothing" (IAG, 64). The new world the Puritans were building was made by their own hands, "shrewdly working," but it is precisely this knowledge which is mystified by their ideology. Displacing power and autonomy to an absent center, nostalgically yearning after nothingness, they can pro- ceed to "deceive themselves and all the despoiled of the world into their sorry beliefs." And once the pattern has been established, by words like those of Cotton Mather, it persists even down to those later Puritans who, bewildered among their machines and believing them- selves to be empty, seek to obey a distant center.

In the American Grain is itself a historicizing text to the extent that it allows the reader to become aware of a variety of different language usages and then to see those linguistic differences as in each case grounded in history. Each one represents an alternative way of mastering specific physical and social conditions, whether of initial colonization, frontier expansion, or industrial organization. Thrown together as they are by Williams, they recall the contentiousness and the uncertainty of history, rather than the smooth inevitability of the classroom history text. Williams argues that the imposition of what he refers to as the "premise that serves to fix us" depends on drawing lines which mark out a figure from its (subsequently) invisible ground— effacing Burr's nobler motives from historical memory by imposing a different figure, of the unstable egotist, for example. It would follow, then, that the action which destroys the illusion that such a figure is natural or total must attack the lines which inscribe it. Stephen J. Greenblatt has described the imposition of colonial power on the New World in terms which are particularly illuminating when set beside Williams's earlier account. Greenblatt uses the term "improvisation" in arguing that "what is essential is the Europeans' ability again and again to insinuate themselves into the preexisting political, religious, even psychic, structures of the natives and to turn those structures to their advantage."[16] The key to this process is the ability to play a role, and "such role playing in turn depends upon the transformation of another's reality into manipulable fiction." To see a pattern as fiction is to see the lines which have constituted it, and that done, the pattern may be destroyed, or appropriated for new ends. For Williams, language has drawn the lines which shaped America's beginnings, and his method in *In the American Grain* was to insinuate himself into the styles which governed history, to fictionalize them, and so to end the Hamiltonian regime of ever more centralized control by revealing it to be a thing made, a construct of men seeking power.

The counter principle which Williams opposes to the American tradition which he regards as responsible for the degradation of his own time, however, raises questions very similar to those which I discussed in relation to D. H. Lawrence. *In the American Grain* is strongly reminiscent of Lawrence's nearly contemporary *Studies in Classic American Literature*. Both writers ascribed the destructive element in American society to an instrumental reason which confined and limited autonomy—Williams's Hamiltonian treadmill, as an image for industrial mechanization, was Lawrence's "millions of squirrels running in millions of cages."[17] But like Lawrence, Williams sought an alternative to the constraining tradition of Hamilton and the Puritans through images of organic vitality. Even the form of his book has been described as organic. Linda Wagner, for example, has called it "Williams' great testimony to the efficacy of organic form in prose as well as in poetry," a judgment which follows from her characterization of his poetic theory of "organic form, the art object as a machine made of words, searching for its own autonymous shape."[18] While Wagner emphasizes stylistic wholeness and self-integration at the expense of other senses of her double metaphor of an organic-machine, my own emphasis has been on the ways in which Williams calls attention to the ventriloquism of his text, revealing the contingency and the artificiality of historical discourse. But notions of the organic and the natural did have a powerful appeal for Williams, and to ignore them would be to give a very distorted picture of his writing.

Aaron Burr is described as "profligate" and "irregular," and Williams notes that he is said to have kept ten women and to have had a hundred bastard children. Père Sebastian Rasles, the French priest who lived with the Indians of Maine, is another of Williams's figures of excess (though not in this case sexual excess). He is explicitly set against Mather and the Puritan need to "have closed all the world out," especially the Indian, who is seen by Mather as only an "unformed Puritan." Rasles, on the contrary, is described in terms of an endlessly productive generosity: "And to give to him who HAS, who will join, who will make, who will fertilize, who will be like you yourself: to create, to hybridize, to crosspollenize,—not to sterilize, to draw back, to fear, to dry up, to rot" (IAG, 121). By living with the Indians, touching them, he becomes a figure of openness, in contrast not only to Mather but to such men as Ben Franklin, who is pictured as "the dike keeper, keeping out the wilderness with his wits." When Williams defines the destructive element in the American tradition, he tends to use images of the man-made: walls, dikes, waterwheels. But when he proposes an alternative, his images are organic: Rasles's cross-pollenizing, or Burr, in whom "there burned a springtime of the soul" (IAG, 196). Daniel Boone, another of Williams's heroes, has only "to be *himself* in a new world, Indian-like" (IAG, 137). The Indian whom Boone must resemble is "a natural expression of the place, the Indian himself as 'right,' the flower of his world."

As I noted earlier, Williams occasionally employed language which, like that of Lawrence, unwittingly reproduced key assumptions of the industrial modernity which he opposed. It is precisely when he turns to the kind of organic metaphors described above that the import of his social criticism becomes less clear. Like Lawrence, Williams offered a critique which historicizes the condition of advanced industrial societies very concretely and precisely. But the solution which he proposed to the oppressions of industrial rationalization and centralization is one which tends to abandon historical analysis in favor of metaphysical notions of essence: whatever "himself" is, it was always there, waiting to emerge like the oak tree in the acorn. But if we are what we are because we have been "fixed" by the premises of discourse, of a closed and interested history writing, as Williams argues in "The Virtue of History," then we must contend with those fixing discourses as they are reproduced within our own historical moment. To suggest that we might simply flower naturally in the wilderness, once all civilization has been left behind, is, to the contrary, a profoundly ahistorical position.

When Williams says that it is impossible for Americans to recognize themselves "until someone invent the ORIGINAL terms" (226), he instructs us to read his mosaic of imitated styles as an account of the historical constraints on the present and an invitation to recover our lost autonomy through the reappropriation of language. But when his organic metaphors suggest that we turn away from language and history and seek some kind of inner springtime, or rebirth, he undermines the social import of his own textual strategy of juxtaposing multiple discourses. And more to the point, he acquiesces in society's separation of literary knowledge—conceived as the knowledge of eternal truths—from that practical knowledge which builds dams and establishes industries. If Williams falters in this way in prescribing a cure for the social ills he diagnoses so acutely, he only illustrates the enormous difficulty which all the modernists faced in their need to employ a language which had already been thoroughly appropriated into the sphere of industrial modernity.

Chapter 6

Nature and Work
In *Paterson*

———————————————— **I** ————————————————

There is little ambiguity in Williams's attitude toward the contemporary discourse of instrumental knowledge which had so narrowed the working lives and the self-understanding of the men and women who were his perennial subjects: he was its implacable enemy. But his views on how art, including his own poetry, should respond to the dangers of an increasingly technological society are more complex. The difficulties raised by his own artistic practice may be suggested, in part, by his comments on other artists. Charles Sheeler, for example, was a painter greatly admired by Williams, and in his most familiar choice of subject—the industrial landscape—an artist whose work is directly related to the question of what stance art should adopt with regard to the industrial context of modernity.

In his *Autobiography,* Williams uses Sheeler's life as well as his painting in a discussion (based on Charles Olson's notion of projective verse) of the need to "reconstruct" the modern poem. In order to support his assertion that "the poem is made of things—on a field,"[1] he sets up a series of equivalences, including poems, paintings, Sheeler's recent marriage, and an old house in the Hudson River Valley to which he and his new bride have just moved. What Williams seeks to emphasize in this extended play of metaphor is the layer upon layer of historical reality which should be a part of any poem as much as it is a part of Sheeler's house. Poems should not be smooth and synthesizing historical generalizations, but archaeological records, the accretion of materials which continue to preserve their mutual differences.

Sheeler moves into a gardener's cottage on an estate of the early colonial aristocracy, an estate which had been altered by the new wealth of subsequent decades. The echoes of Washington Irving's country are there, along with European architecture, a beautiful collection of ornamental trees, a lost tobacco fortune, and the memory of the main house destroyed out of spite toward Franklin Roosevelt. Moreover, the individual histories of a bride driven out of Russia by the Revolution, and of Sheeler's own Welsh father and Pennsylvania background are also a part of the poem/ painting/ life: "The poem (in Charles's case the painting) is the construction in understandable limits of his life." The house as something made up of many kinds of preexisting materials is Williams's central image: "The house that they have set up (I continue to refer to the construction, the reconstitution of the poem as my major theme) is the present-day necessity."[2] This notion of the "constructed" work of art would seem to imply the kind of historicizing gesture which I ascribed to *In the American Grain*, insofar as that work invites examination of the "raw materials" of history, the contending discourses which had not yet been swallowed up into invisibility by a totalizing History.

But this reading of Sheeler, which sees the presence of history in his work as intractably material, resistant to generalization, should be placed beside that of Leo Marx. In *The Machine in the Garden*, Marx discusses one of Sheeler's paintings of contemporary industry, "American Landscape":

> No trace of untouched nature remains. Not a tree or a blade of grass is in view. The water is enclosed by man-made banks, and the sky is filling with smoke. Like the reflection upon the water, every natural object represents some aspect of the collective economic enterprise. Technological power overwhelms the solitary man; the landscape convention calls for his presence to provide scale, but here the traditional figure acquires new meaning: in this mechanized environment he seems forlorn and powerless. And yet, somehow, this bleak vista conveys a strangely soft, tender feeling. On closer inspection, we observe that Sheeler has eliminated all evidence of the frenzied movement and clamor we associate with the industrial scene.[3]

The double-take which Marx enacts in this passage is meant to define the contradictory effects which such a painting produces: the perception of industrialization rendering mankind weak and powerless at first, but then the fading away of social criticism into aesthetic effect: "This 'American Landscape' is the industrial landscape pastoralized. By superimposing order, peace, and harmony upon our modern chaos, Sheeler represents the anomalous blend of illusion and reality in the American consciousness."[4]

A similar point about Williams himself has been made by Bram Dijkstra. He argues that Williams's work demonstrates the way in which a society "exerts ideological control over its artists" by driving them "away from genuine historical consciousness and into an artificial 'avant-gardist' rebellion against immediately preceding periods." Dijkstra concludes that "no matter how loudly Williams might protest, as he does in his article on Sheeler, that the world of the artist is 'the world in which men meet and work with pick and shovel, talk and write long winded books. It is the same world we go to war in,' he in actuality never chose to confront that world in other than its visual textures, in its surface modulations."[5] A judgment of this sort is important because it is so characteristic of the kind of criticism of modernist writers (by critics such as Lukács, for example) which assumes a causal link between three crucial elements: "avant-gardist" interest in technical innovation, an aestheticist concern for formal, surface qualities, and the abandonment of any social engagement or historical consciousness.

What it means to "confront" the world of work is the difficult question. Certainly, in his essays on Sheeler, Williams did acknowledge the realities of industrialization: "Inhuman is a word commonly used to describe the efficiency of the modern industrial setup, as in some minds coldness is often associated with Sheeler's work—incorrectly. Sheeler chose as he did from temperament doubtless but also from thought and a clear vision of the contemporary dilemma." While industrial efficiency is a concept with quite specific historical referents, "dilemma" is a word which may either help to describe a historical situation or blur its historicity by suggesting something much more metaphysical: the "human condition" in a contemporary version. Williams's prose does not resolve the ambiguity:

> Sheeler is a painter first and last with a painter's mind alert to the significance of the age which surrounds him. The emotional power of his work comes also from that. It is hard to believe that a picture such as *Classic Landscape*, which is a representation of the Ford plant at River Rouge, owes its effectiveness to an arrangement of cylinders and planes in the distance, maybe it isn't entirely that but that contributes to it largely. It is, however it comes about, a realization on the part of the artist of man's pitiful weakness and at the same time his fate in the world.[6]

The delineation of specific historical causes for "man's pitiful weakness" in the modern age is possible, and Williams did attempt it—in stories about workers so cowed by management that they were even afraid to complain about serious injuries, or in essays about the domination of instrumental reason over science, education, and literary publishing. But that is not the same thing as the depiction of "fate,"

that metaphysical counter which renders historical causality unnecessary. And neither historical nor metaphysical causes are equivalent to
the aesthetic appreciation of planes and cylinders as a principle of
artistic organization.

The possibility that Williams treated the realm of modern work
much as Sheeler is alleged to have done, that is, that he described it only
to retreat once again into an ahistorical pastoralism, has serious implications for any reading of his major works, and particularly for *Paterson*.
I have already argued that a work such as *In the American Grain* proposes
organic spontaneity and wholeness as a possible salvation from the historical degradations which it depicts so clearly. A myth of Nature thus
persists in that book's more traditional elements—its metaphors and its
descriptions of character, for example. But at the same time, a contrary,
historicizing tendency may be found in other textual features of the book,
principally in its innovative strategy of juxtaposing multiple styles, each
one a distinctive social discourse, grounded in history.

In its representation of a multitude of languages, from early
American newspaper conventions to 1920s working-class slang, *Paterson* exhibits formal innovations which are similar to those of *In the
American Grain*, but once again, form—in this case "open form"—
cannot bear meaning in and of itself. In pointing out an ambiguity
between the historicizing tendency of *In the American Grain*, on the
one hand, and its quite different, mythic-organic use of language, on
the other, I would indicate that two discursive patterns are at work in
Williams's writing, each with a distinct social import and each contra-
dicting the other. This is not an argument about the "undecidability" of
language in Williams's texts, however, but an attempt to question the
ideological premises which underlie those texts.

I make this distinction because the notion of undecidability has
been important to recent criticism of Williams. Marjorie Perloff, for
example, has written about works such as *Kora in Hell* and *Spring and
All* using the notion of undecidability to show how Williams, like
certain other artists in the tradition of Rimbaud, destabilizes the
relation of signifier to signified, making it impossible to read these
works as coherent symbolic discourse. Distinguishing her position
from that of Derrida, however, Perloff sees indeterminacy not as a
characteristic of all texts, but as a particular literary strategy, one
among many. Thus *Spring and All* is a work characterized by undecidability, while later works such as *Paterson* and "Asphodel, that Greeny
Flower," are not. She regards *Paterson* as in fact a return to the
Symbolist tradition, and therefore as "a much more 'closed' poem than
either Williams or his best critics care to admit."[7]

The most uncompromising argument about *Paterson's* undecidability has been offered by Joseph N. Riddel. He sees Williams engaging in "a play of language which undoes all myths of a last (res)erec-

tion," breaking the illusion that words can recover an origin which is at once ontological essence and sexual seed. Riddel argues that Williams turns myth into fiction and so unweaves or opens it, relying on deconstructive insights into the undecidability of language itself: "The classical dream of an inert, referential and representational, language is undone by the very act (writing) of poetic arrangement, which always involves a rearrangement, and hence a reinscription, of words from the contexts where they seem to function referentially (literally): that is, to be nonderivative. It is this transfer or displacement which unleashes the dissonance of the word, or its own metaphorical instability. If writing can only represent this instability, it represents the undoing of a classical dream of reflexivity."[8]

If the double inscription which Riddel traces through *Paterson* issues in a freeplay that shatters the nostalgic myth of recovering lost origins, it nevertheless seems to exist forever at this point of beginning. In *The Inverted Bell* he writes of *Paterson*, Book 1, that it was "a book of Genesis," a metapoem which, in turning language upon itself, returned to language's primordial roots; while of Book 5 he writes that it was "a dance of beginnings, a Dionyssian rout, a breaking up of the sacred unity into an original difference, a first measure."[9] In Chapter 2, I discussed his analysis of Pound's verse, and I would point to the similarity of his conclusions about Williams: once liberated from both the traditional logocentric myth and the Modernist lament at discovering an absent center, poetry emerges into a realm of difference which is strangely like a freeze frame: poised in tension and potentiality, but still. Language's initial transgression is suddenly everywhere, but history never begins. Thus in his later article on Book Five, Riddel constructs a brilliant account of the museum as a scene of representation, a border, and yet his deconstruction makes no move to get beyond the initiating space of difference: "The scene of the museum is a scene of borders representing borders. Nothing is, strictly, inside a border; or outside."[10] But borders define patterns—or to use Williams's terms, "the premises that fix us." They inscribe society's systems of knowledge, belief, and value, and we ignore them only at the cost of further mystifying the ideologies that constrain every man and woman.

II

Paterson constructs an argument about the idea of constraint and divorce in industrial society, but that argument is built on the concrete detail of its characters' lives. The mindless vulgarity of picnickers in the park, for example, elicits a generalization:

Minds beaten thin
by waste—among

the working classes SOME sort
of breakdown
has occurred. Semi-roused

they lie upon their blanket
face to face,
mottled by the shadows of the leaves

upon them, unannoyed,
at least here unchallenged.
Not undignified . . .[11]

This passage follows a description of a particularly skimpy bikini, but Williams does not ascribe the breakdown which has occurred among the working classes to a simple decline in taste. Sunday in the park has become the only time in which they are not challenged, as personal fulfillment becomes radically separated from the sheer instrumentality of their roles at work. Williams names the two greatest human costs which the workers must pay for Taylorized industry: the reduction of their own dignity, and the waste of their minds, as the mental components of work are withdrawn to the province of management.

From the point of view of management, one of the most desirable consequences of the newly designed worker was a predictable uniformity. Skilled workers in the nineteenth century had tended to change jobs very frequently, and in great numbers, and the vagrancy laws of the turn of the century had been one attempt to limit this disruptive individuality on the part of the working class. But far more effective was to take away the leverage which their detailed knowledge of industrial crafts gave them over management, by transforming them into interchangeable parts, easily replaced:

At the

sanitary lunch hour packed woman to
woman (or man to woman, what's the difference?)
the flesh of their faces gone
to fat or gristle, without recognizable
outline, fixed in rigors, adipose or sclerosis
expressionless, facing one another, a mould
for all faces (canned fish) this .

Move toward the back, please, and face the door!

is how the money's made,
money's made

(P, 196)

And like Pound and Ford, Williams makes clear that the transformation of workers into indistinguishable canned fish was equally true of office work:

> While in the tall
> buildings (sliding up and down) is where
> the money's made
>   up and down
>   directed missiles
> in the greased shafts of the tall buildings   .
> They stand torpid in cages, in violent motion
> unmoved
>   but alert!
>   predatory minds, un-
> affected
>   UNINCONVENIENCED
>   unsexed, up
> and down (without wing motion) This is how
> the money's made . using such plugs.
>   (P, 195)

Even sexual identity is obliterated as these men and women become simply "plugs." In Book 5, Williams employs a contrast with the past to define the sheer emptiness of such people: "It is no mortal sin to be poor—anything but this featureless tribe that has the money now—staring into the atom, completely blind—without grace or pity, as if they were so many shellfish. The artist, Brueghel, saw them   .   :   the suits of his peasants were of better stuff, hand woven, than we can boast" (P, 265).

Williams uses the technique of contrasting old and new ways to define a range of consequences following from the loss of the worker's control over the work process. On the one hand, there is a deterioration in the quality of the products themselves: "—have come in our time to the age of shoddy, the men are shoddy, driven by their bosses, inside and outside the job to be done, at a profit. To whom? But not true of the Portuguese mason, his own boss 'in the new country' who is building a wall for me, moved by the oldworld knowledge of what is 'virtuous' " (P, 266). Far more sinister, however, is the human degeneration which leads to the "$40-a-week factory worker" in Book 4, who fractures his baby's skull by snapping the tray of her high chair in her face (P, 229). This account is juxtaposed with an anecdote about an old Dutch farmer who demonstrates far more concern for mere horses, protecting his team from the danger of a cholera epidemic by leaving them outside the town and carrying his goods to market himself, in a wheelbarrow.

As he has done in *In the American Grain*, Williams uses the historical anecdote both as a rhetorical device to criticize the present and as a way of constructing a historical explanation for the shape which that present has assumed. Once again, Alexander Hamilton takes his place as a man whose institutional programs were directly related to the diminished dignity, autonomy, and mental scope of the modern worker. Hamilton proceeded from a premise which necessarily led to centralized organization, rather than to the decentralization of knowledge and power: "He never trusted the people, 'a great beast,' as he saw them and held Jefferson to be little better if not worse than any" (P, 84). The institutional scheme for realizing this centralization was the Society for Useful Manufactures (S.U.M.), located around the waterpower of Paterson, and Williams summarizes that scheme much as he had in *In the American Grain*. The Federal Writer's Project volume from which Williams drew the passages about Hamilton and the S.U.M. notes that Paterson "was a company town, and its workers began to exhibit signs of dissatisfaction. S.U.M. records tells [sic] of 'disorderly' calico printers as early as 1794. This resulted in the closing of the mill—the first lock-out in American history and the forerunner of a long string of industrial struggles." Conditions in the textile mills of Paterson are in fact described as exceptionally harsh, and the volume's authors point out that "over the years, the embattled textile workers of Paterson and Passaic have become the State's symbol of resistance to exploitation."[12] In the years immediately preceding the First World War, the long history of the textile mills became still more complicated, as a New Jersey cotton mill became one of the first industries beyond metalworking to apply the principles of scientific management and, moreover, to apply them to women's work.[13]

Even more fundamental than Paterson's specific history of labor resistance on the one side and continual management innovations on the other, however, was a general cultural mentality which subordinated all other considerations to the generation of profits. For Williams, the instrumental reason of the twentieth century was rooted in an earlier American willingness to regard man or beast alike as faceless Other, and to destroy them if necessary, in order to become rich. Like the Dutch colonists who dig up the body of a dead Indian in order to steal the furs in which he had been buried, the settlers of Book 1 destroy millions of mussels in a frenzied search for pearls. But by the twentieth century, the creation of wealth was not simply a question of reaping nature's bounty—cracking mussel shells, or clubbing eels in a drained reservoir. The appropriation of knowledge to the ends of practical work was the key to the most recent attempts to increase productivity. Taylorism, most notably, involved (in John Dos Passos's words) the "gathering in on the part of those on the management's side all the great mass of traditional knowledge which in the past has been in the heads of the workmen."[14]

In *Paterson*, it is a withdrawing of knowledge from ordinary working men and women which accounts for much of the emptiness of modern life. All of the constraining discourses which shape the lives of the poem's characters are, finally, restrictions of knowledge:

> Who restricts knowledge? Some say
> it is the decay of the middle class
> making an impossible moat between the high
> and the low where
> the life once flourished . . knowledge
> of the avenues of information—
> So that we do not know (in time)
> where the stasis lodges. And if it is not
> the knowledgeable idiots, the university,
> they at least are the non-purveyors
> should be devising means
> to leap the gap. Inlets? The outward
> masks of the special interests
> that perpetuate the stasis and make it
> profitable.
>
> (P, 46)

Passing quickly over the magazine sociology of middle-class "decay," Williams sees a process which is structural rather than organic. There is a widening gap between the segments of a society characterized by increasingly hierarchical relations. But that gap is constituted by a disruption in the flow of information, which is withheld from the many as a way of ensuring the power and profits of the few.

> Cash is mulct of them that others may live
> secure
> . .   and knowledge restricted.
> An orchestral dullness overlays their world.
>
> (P, 78)

Even the universities have failed to interfere with the profitable new use of knowledge, as they tacitly support the paradigm by turning it upside down, and accepting their own powerlessness as "knowledgeable idiots."

In Book 3, Williams constructs a sequence which makes clear not only the pervasiveness of instrumental reason in his world, but also the way in which his opposition to that degradation of knowledge leads to his sometimes ambiguous sympathy for both workers and owners. Lambert, an English immigrant who became wealthy as a Paterson mill owner, and who "was the first/ to oppose the unions," represents management by sheer will, or even personal whim:

> This is MY shop. I reserve the right (and he did)
> to walk down the row (between his looms) and
> fire any son-of-a-bitch I choose without excuse
> or reason more than that I don't like his face.
>
> (P, 121)

Lambert's highly individualistic style of management was common in the earlier stages of the industrial revolution, but it was entirely contrary to the newer assumptions of scientific management. A key aim of Taylor's system was achieving cooperation between labor and management by demonstrating to the workers that what they were being asked to do was determined by scientific law, not the mere whims of an employer. In his scheme, both employer and employee were to recognize their common interest by acknowledging the rule of science in all areas of planning and production. Taylor himself had no use for the sort of unenlightened management practiced by Lambert.

But in the poem (as in history), it was the assumptions of scientific management, not the idiosyncratic will of a self-made millionaire, which prevailed. Lambert ultimately failed, and the elaborate mansion which he had built was scheduled for demolition:

> The "Castle" too to be razed. So be it. For no
> reason other than that it is *there*, in-
> comprehensible; of no USE! So be it. So be it.

Reason which is not directed to some practical goal outside itself has become no reason at all, under the new order of knowledge; neither a castle nor a management decision can simply *be*.

But the imperative of USE has also affected the union movement which in its opposition seems to reflect the same changes which have transformed management. Williams quotes from a letter which he had received in response to Book 2: "Rose and I didn't know each other when we both went to the Paterson strike around the first war and worked in the Pagent. She went regularly to feed Jack Reed in jail and I listened to Big Bill Heywood, Gurley Flynn and the rest of the big hearts and helping hands in Union Hall. And look at the damned thing now" (P, 122). Referring to the Paterson textile strike of 1913, led by the IWW, the letter contrasts that moment of personal involvement by highly individual and committed labor leaders to what is presumably the subsequent degeneration of the union movement. Through characters like Joe Stecher in the novels, Williams had often expressed the view that unions had sold out their idealistic commitments in order to embrace instead a principle of expediency which was little different than the ruthless instrumentality of business. Williams's opposition was thus to a broad cultural discourse, as much as it was to the actions of specific groups within society.

Viewed against this background of broad social change, Williams's use of the notion of "divorce" appears more complex than it does in the standard readings which emphasize a loss of organic wholeness or the disciplinary divisions of universities:[15]

> Divorce is
> the sign of knowledge in our time,
> divorce! divorce!

Williams saw that knowledge could only be constituted in its present form (primarily scientific, administered by an elite group, and authorized by its usefulness to industry) through many acts of divorce, all serving to differentiate this new, restricted field of knowledge from that which was now nonknowledge, and from those who were to be excluded from participation in its power. In *The Embodiment of Knowledge* he had rejected the notion "that humanity is split and of two kinds."[16] But he had found it necessary to consider and reject that most radical kind of division of the human subject because of the apparent triumph within industrial society of a discourse of expertise from which ordinary men and women were increasingly excluded.

III

When Williams challenged industrial rationalization, he did so on the basis of its human consequences, especially its tendency to fragment the human subject. This approach to the question of economic change is partly responsible for the ambiguity of his political identifications. Although he was generally sympathetic to the left, he was suspicious of both the Communist and Fascist alternatives which were presented to him during the 1930s. Williams's attempt to find a middle ground which still allowed radical cultural critique, rather than simply liberal tolerance, might be better understood in light of Philip Rahv's analysis, in 1950, of the American intellectual climate. Rahv made a distinction between the utopians of the right and those of the left, based on their respective attitudes toward the human subject.[17] While the leftists assumed the innate goodness of man—naively, according to Rahv—those on the right held that man had "a fixed human nature that is innately evil," a position which was equally unacceptable because it could be used to justify "man's inhumanity to man."

Rahv referred to the proponents of these two positions as "futurists" and "archaists," respectively, regarding both views as idealisms which effectively closed history to human intervention. His own proposal avoided either extreme: "The dissident artist, if he understands the extremity of the age and voices what it tries to stifle, will thus be saved from its corruption. Instead of deceiving himself and others—either by playing with bureaucratized visions of the shining cities of the future or by turning his art into a shrine for things that are dead and gone—he would be faithful to the metamorphosis of the present."[18] There is an ambiguity in the choice of "metamorphosis,"

which can be taken either to denote an action—changing the present—
or simply to describe the present as a time of openness and change.
When he wrote about Dostoevsky as "the first novelist to have fully
accepted and dramatized the principle of uncertainty or indeterminacy in the presentation of character," he employed both meanings,
viewing Dostoevsky's art as a response to a preexisting condition of
modernity, but a response which, in its technical innovation, was itself
an active intervention into that historical situation.[19] He speaks of
"Dostoevsky's acute awareness (self-awareness at bottom) of the prob-
lematical nature of the modern personality and of its tortuous efforts
to stem the disintegration threatening it."

Elsewhere, Rahv argued, against the efforts of those intellectuals
who would solve the disintegration by recovering ancient myth, that "it
is the paradox of progress that humanity has proven itself unable to
assimilate reality except by means of 'the alienation of human forces.'
In order to recover the potency of myth civilized man would first have
to undo the whole of his history."[20] The alternative is to confront the
reality of disintegration as it exists in the present, and that means to
confront the consequences of industrialization:

> What Marx once called "the idiocy of the division of labor" must have
> gone very far indeed if people can so drastically separate their
> theories of life from their concrete living of it! (The "idiocy" results
> from the fragmentation of vital human functions, since, as Marx said,
> "together with the division of labor is given the possibility, nay, the
> actuality, that spiritual activity and material activity, pleasure and
> work, production and consumption, will fall to the lot of different
> individuals.")

The challenge which Rahv made to contemporary artists was thus a
double one: to depict the fragmentation of human functions in the
industrialized world without retreating into idealized myths of past or
future, but at the same time to intervene in that fragmentation through
artistic inventions like that of Dostoevsky's indeterminacy of character.
The open form of *Paterson*, as a poetic equivalent for Dostoevsky's
novelistic devices, is the vehicle for the poem's potential intervention
into social order. Historical specificity does not lie in the form itself,
however, but in Williams's use of the form to represent, and demystify,
the multiple social discourses which shape identity in the modern
world, but shape it as fragmented and partial. Williams depicts the
considerable range into which those discourses claiming to define the
human can fall. There is the utter materialism of science, for example:

> The body is tilted slightly forward from the basic standing
> position and the weight thrown on the ball of the foot,
> while the other thigh is lifted and the leg and opposite
> arm are swung forward (fig. 6B). Various muscles, aided   .
> (P, 59)

But this example of authorless scientific prose is juxtaposed with the highly self-aware, even neurotic language of the age of psychoanalysis: "Despite my having said that I'd never write to you again, I do so now because I find, with the passing of time, that the outcome of my failure with you has been the complete damming up of all my creative capacities in a particularly disastrous manner such as I have never experienced" (P, 59). Radical inwardness and radical objectivity each possess their own distinctive syntax and vocabulary. When placed together, as Williams does in this passage, each tends to make the other seem a parody of itself.

If these two languages represent men and women as either mechanism or subjectivity, other powerful discourses seek to create a self-identity which is entirely independent of the material world. This is Klaus Ehrens, preaching to the poor about the value of poverty:

> I couldn't eat, I couldn't
> sleep for thinking of my trouble so that
> when the Lord came to me the third time I was
> ready and I kneeled down before Him
> and said, Lord, do what you will with me!
> Give away your money, He said, and I
> will make you the richest man in the world!
> And I bowed my head and said to Him, Yea, Lord.
> And His blessed truth descended upon me and filled
> me with joy, such joy and such riches as I
> had never in my life known to that day and I said
> to Him, Master!

The social repressiveness of this kind of evangelical language is made explicit in Book 4, as Billy Sunday's rhetorical powers are shown to be worth money to management, during a strike:

> He's *on*
> the table now! Both feet, singing
> (a foot song) his feet canonized .
> .   as paid for
> by the United Factory Owners' Ass'n   .
> . to "break" the strike
> and put those S.O.B.s in their places, be
> Geezus, by calling them to God!
> (P, 203)

The United Factory Owners's use of Billy Sunday is a deliberate attempt to manipulate the workers, but much of what Williams depicts as modern subjectivity is the result of a more generalized condition of restricted knowledge, of "minds beaten thin/ by waste." More than anything else, it is a trivialization of consciousness: "Dear B. Please excuse me for not having told you this when I was over to your house. I had no courage to answer your questions so I'll write it. Your dog *is* going to have puppies although I prayed she would be okay. It wasn't that she was left alone as she never was but I used to let her out at dinner time while I hung up my clothes . . . Don't think I haven't been worrying about Musty. She's occupied my mind every day since that awful event" (P, 69). The propensity to think in diminutives, to adopt a childlike overinvestment in small dogs, is one kind of compensation for minds cut off from what society has defined as the only kind of serious work—that is, practical and profitable work.

What Williams describes is a set of assumptions which not only trivialize personal identity, but which effectively disenfranchise all forms of thought or expression which are not instrumental to the present economic order. Literature too becomes a lapdog in this trivializing discourse:

> For the writing
> is also an attack and means must be
>
> found to scotch it—at the root
> if possible. So that
>
> to write, nine tenths of the problem
> is to live. They see
>
> to it, not by intellection but
> by sub-intellection (to want to be
>
> blind as a pretext for
> saying, We're so proud of you!
>
> A wonderful gift! How *do*
> you find the time for it in
>
> your busy life? It must be a great
> thing to have such a pastime.
> (P, 137f.)

Once again, the process of "sub-intellection" operates through a distinctive language, which in this case is constituted by such features as multiple exclamation points and the heavy reliance on patronizing cliches.

If literature is allowed to be reduced to no more than a "pastime," it can surely offer little threat to the instrumental reason of the workplace, and Williams accordingly reserves his harshest judgments for those who should preserve the critical potential of thought (artists and intellectuals, for example), but who fail to do so. The universities are a prime area of misplaced trust:

> we go on living, we permit ourselves
> to continue—but certainly
> not for the university, what they publish

severally or as a group: clerks
got out of hand forgetting for the most part
to whom they are beholden.

spitted on fixed concepts like
roasting hogs, sputtering, their drip sizzling
in the fire

(P, 44)

Like the "fixed premises" of *In the American Grain*, the "fixed concepts" of *Paterson* represent acquiescence to forces which would constitute men and women as interchangeable agents of industrial production, on the one hand, and as trivialized consumers, on the other. As the archive for these various fixities, the library in *Paterson* becomes a place of "desolation," and Williams describes it as possessing a smell of "stagnation and death" (P, 123). Williams conceives cultural institutions (libraries, universities, literary publishing) not as autonomous, but as "beholden." In the passage above, it is presumably the "people" to whom the universities are beholden, but they have evidently forgotten their debt, and a page later the actual allegiance of the university is said to be to "the special interests."

The fixed concepts of the professors and the stagnating record of those concepts in libraries drive the poet at one point to ask for relief from "meaning" (135). The quotation marks do not question the notion of meaning itself, but rather they underline the historically bound and interested condition of meaning which Williams must confront in his world. He used a similar tactic in *The Embodiment of Knowledge*, where he spoke of two kinds of "truth" but only placed one in quotation marks:

> But by breaking up formulas would we not be merely losing sight of fixed truths which we need for our continued intellectual existence, would we not be reverting to nonsense without any compensatory gain—even were it possible to break up language to that extent? No. Language is the key to the mind's escape from bondage to the past. There are no "truths" that can be fixed in language. It is by the breakup of the language that the truth can be seen to exist and that it becomes operative again. Such reasoning as Spengler's depends on the fixities of language which it is the purpose of such writers as Joyce and Stein—fail tho' they may in detail—to blast. (EK, 19)

In discussing D. H. Lawrence's attitude toward knowledge, in Chapter 3, I concluded that he had compromised his opposition to industrial oppression by acquiescing in the dominant identification of knowledge with instrumental reason. When he saw literature's salvation as existing in a mythic-organic realm apart from the mundane world of work, he virtually joined Billy Sunday in putting the workers in their places by "calling them to God!" Williams, on the contrary, is not ready to relinquish knowledge and language as proper sites of struggle, any more than he will accept the characterization of poetry writing as an amusing "pastime." When the library burns in Book 3, he does not simply bid good riddance, but equates its smoke with that of sacred Indian ritual, breathing it in in the hope of "warping the sense to detect the norm, to break/ through the skull of custom" (P, 139). Fixed concepts are not to be destroyed; they are to be unfrozen, so to speak, their principles of fixity made visible, so that they may be reappropriated in ways which enable rather than constrain human potentiality.

Defining literature by contrasting it with society's instrumental use of language, without at the same time ending up in an ahistorical impasse, however, is not an easy task. In *The Embodiment of Knowledge*, Williams distinguishes literature from all those other disciplines in which language is subordinate to something outside itself. He says that the function of the province of letters is to "re-enkindle language, to break it away from its enforcements, its prostitutions under all other categories. For language that is used as a means to an end foreign to itself is language used as an expedient—something that cannot be scientifically or philosophically sanctioned—impurely" (EK, 20). Opposition to the contemporary appropriation of language by business and industry can very quickly come to sound like an embrace of art for art's sake. And while not necessarily thinking of the "pure" poetry of the Symbolists, critics have asserted, for example, that "*Paterson* is a major work of art by virtue of what it is, and not primarily because of what it says or means;"[21] or that the poet's "lofty conception of the function of art and its elevation above the mundane world of affairs" allied him with those scientists who disclaim any responsibility for the consequences of their discoveries.[22]

Certainly, *Paterson* does contain moments when art is seen as an end in itself, as when, for example, Jackson Pollock's paint is squeezed "pure from the tube. Nothing else/ is real" (P, 249). But the overwhelming burden of historical detail in the poem speaks a different message. Given *Paterson*'s detailed representation of—and clearly stated opposition to—the powerful economic discourses of the twentieth century, the question is not whether the poem removes itself from history into an autonomous realm of art, but whether, like Lawrence, Williams formulates a counterdiscourse which unwittingly reinforces the assumptions underlying industrial rationalization. For both Williams and Lawrence, the idea of Nature is central to their opposition to industrial society, but it is important to remember that the meaning of Nature is far from simple.

As Raymond Williams has put it, "the idea of nature contains an extraordinary amount of human history."[23] One historical thread, as Raymond Williams notes, is the "sense of nature as the inherent and essential quality of any particular thing" (68), a sense which becomes an important constituent of idealist thought, and which leads to the idea of an essential human nature, which may then be identified with all natural process. Although this is Lawrence's conception of human essence, as a metaphoric seed waiting to flower, the historic significance of his position depends on the way in which it was interpolated into the actual economic and social contentions of the moment. When he used it as a rationale for consigning knowledge to the realm of the merely instrumental, the idea of natural human essence had the effect of supporting the ideology of industrial management.

Lawrence's identification of human beings with Nature was ultimately a version of the "archaism" denounced by Philip Rahv, and it encouraged us to turn away from the malaise of industrialization in search of more "permanent" values. But the contrary perception of nature, as absolutely other than the human, has not just allowed us to ignore the present: it has functioned historically as a powerful justification for the very technological exploitation of the natural world which has created the present. When nature is regarded as a thing apart, it becomes little more than an object for human mastery. If both identifying with nature and distancing oneself from it thus support (either passively or actively) the ideology of technological mastery, then Nature would seem to be a poor choice for anyone seeking a sound basis for opposition. But these two alternatives do not exhaust the possible ways in which the idea of nature may be used to confront concrete historical circumstances.

Raymond Williams points out that a good deal of what we think of as the "natural landscape" is actually the "product of human design and human labour, and in admiring it as natural it matters very much whether we suppress that fact of labour or acknowledge it."[24] He argues that it is essential that men and women once again see themselves as a part of nature, that they see the countless ways in which what we have tended to think of as simply the transformation of nature has always involved the transformation of human lives as well. In Raymond Williams's view, the regime of "abstracted Man" set against "abstracted Nature" is fundamental to aspects of modernity ranging from industrial pollution to "time-and-motion study" (i.e., Taylorism),[25] but the proper alternative lies neither in continuing to accept our separation from nature nor in returning to an atavistic identification with nature-as-myth. It is to be found instead in the recognition that we are indeed a part of nature, but that nature is inseparable from human labor. In short, it is the recovery of historical consciousness.

For Williams the poet of *In the American Grain*, nature did seem to invite a kind of identification which blurred the poem's genuine attempt to attack the mystification of history. But by the time he came to write *Paterson*, Williams had begun to use the idea of nature much more as Raymond Williams has envisioned it, that is, as a way of focusing the reader's attention on historical contention, rather than on timeless natural essence. Eliot's use of seasonal cycles to invoke a mythic notion of salvation through rebirth is explicitly rejected:

> Who is it spoke of April? Some
> insane engineer. There is no recurrence.
> The past is dead.
>> (P, 169)

Throughout the poem, nature is seen through the lens of human action. Most often, the action constitutes exploitation of one sort or another, from the millions of mussels destroyed in search of pearls, to the eels clubbed to death, to the last wolf killed in Paterson. These examples of human assault on nature, which recur throughout the poem, do not exist in isolation; they are invariably connected to the delineation of human history, and specifically to the historical ideology which has issued in the present-day degradation of industrial Paterson. Like Raymond Williams, W. C. Williams regarded industrial pollution and the experience of the working class as related, and related through a discourse which is also shared by the intellectuals:

> Half the river red, half steaming purple
> from the factory vents, spewed out hot,
>
>
> swirling, bubbling. The dead bank,
> shining mud .
>
>
> What can he think else—along
> the gravel of the ravished park, torn by
> the wild workers' children tearing up the grass,
> kicking, screaming? A chemistry, corollary
> to academic misuse, which the theorem
> with accuracy, accurately misses . .
>> (P, 48f.)

In Book 5, Williams includes a letter from Allen Ginsberg which inscribes an image of the young Beat as a noble savage: "When I've seen enough I'll be back to splash in the Passaic again only with a body so naked and happy City Hall will have to call out the Riot Squad" (P, 248). But in an interview, Williams rejected the primitivism of the Beats, remarking that "they can't be primitive. The only thing they can be is more thoughtful than ever."[26] And that remark might serve to describe Williams's poem, which is filled with images of flowers and trees, but which ultimately sees human work, not unconscious flowering, as the way to rebuild the world: "the words will have to be rebricked up" (170). The Ginsberg letter interrupts Williams's extended meditation on the Unicorn Tapestries, a sequence which offers as good an occasion as any to see how he had come to regard the myth of natural innocence.

Although he mentions a frontier myth of the unicorn, what Williams actually describes is a great work of European art which pictures the world of nature as entirely overwritten by human civilization. The Unicorn Tapestries depict a hunting sequence, and they do so with the most careful attention to the details of clothing, weapons, and clearly figured class divisions. In the final panel, which is Williams's main focus, the evidence of human work is everywhere. The unicorn is surrounded by a wooden fence and wears a beautifully embroidered collar around his neck. From the collar, a chain fastens the unicorn to a tree, from which is suspended a large iconographic initial. Like the river red with dye from the silk factories, or the eels dead in the mud, the unicorn we see in these tapestries, and in *Paterson,* is an emblem of history, not its effacement. Nature was not a wilderness of unconscious instinct for Williams: it was the occasion to be more thoughtful than ever.

Chapter 7

At the Edge of Modernity:
Leopold Bloom Wonders

_____ **I** _____

When, in my introduction, I described Frederick Taylor's program of scientific management, I said that I would not simply be tracing the influence of a "great man." "Taylorism" denotes not a single theory, but rather a number of associated practices, ranging from technical procedures for machining steel, to time and motion studies, to recommendations about pay incentives, to philosophical generalizations about the relevance of scientific "law" to economic production. The scientific management movement was assembled by many hands, and it has continued long after Taylor's death. While Taylor was the movement's most energetic salesman, his most distinctive invention was still his initial idea of attempting to find out whether an optimum speed and pressure for cutting any given metal could be determined scientifically. That project depended on the specific application of a more general idea: that science should be of practical use. And it is less important to know where such an idea might have originated than it is to understand how widely it is to be found throughout the industrialized world, and how, in specific circumstances, it has become the object of struggle between those who would make it serve exclusive societal interests and those who would oppose such appropriation. For Taylor, bending science to the imperative of use made possible a new system of industrial management, while for a writer like William Carlos Williams, tracing the destructiveness of instrumental reason, through the history of an old industrial city, became the literary work of decades.

Ireland, as a metropolitan colony of the British Empire which is at once central to, and distant from, the developments of advanced capitalism, can serve well to illustrate the pervasiveness of modernity's discourse of instrumental reason. And as one of the most productive sites of literary modernism, it can also indicate yet another kind of engagement between a modernist artist and the economic realities of the early twentieth century. Still, when *Ulysses* is discussed in the context of the twentieth century, it is generally seen as an exemplary work of experimental fiction, a testimony to the formal preoccupations of international modernism. That this novel, to say nothing of its country of origin, should teach us anything about the economic, technological, and managerial developments of advanced capitalism, which were transforming lives throughout Europe and North America, seems an unlikely prospect. But Ireland, for all its agrarian mystique, was not an isolated preserve. Industrialization in the north had been a reality (political as well as economic) for well over a hundred years, while the greatest industrial powers of the time had found in Ireland a ready supply of workers, who, from the factories of Manchester or Pittsburgh, retained close ties with their homeland. Scholars attempting to understand the cultural context of early twentieth century Irish literature have begun recently to explore the role which Ireland has played in a network of social and economic relations within the British Empire, as well as within the broader realm of advanced capitalist development.

In this vein, W. J. McCormack has recently argued that "Ireland is less a backward and marginal culture than it is a central if repressed area of British modernism. An area of *British* modernism by virtue of its place in the British colonial system, of British *modernism* by virtue of its intimate place in the United Kingdom, the flagship of high capitalism in the nineteenth century." He chides historians for devoting too much attention to such economic activities as cattle raising and shipbuilding, while neglecting the intangible, but powerful, area of ideology: "It is much to the point, both critically and politically, to insist on the problematic nature of literature in the productions we call Anglo-Irish relations and to emphasize the extent to which the metropolitan colony within the United Kingdom of Great Britain and Ireland was devoted to the manufacture of ideology."[1] Extending to cultural affairs the Marxist notion that capitalism requires uneven economic development within its sphere, McCormack is primarily interested in the Literary Revival's creation of a mythic Ireland of traditional peasants and ancient heroes. That familiar Yeatsian myth functions, in relation to the tensions of the industrialized world, much as did the nature mysticism of D. H. Lawrence, which I described earlier: political opposition is displaced by an aesthetic, or quasi-religious, quietism.

While I would agree that the myth making of the Irish Renaissance tends to function in the way McCormack describes (at least in the work of Yeats), it is also true that the world of advanced capitalism was present in Ireland in more direct ways. Although the direction of his own argument does not permit him to develop it, McCormack makes an observation which is particularly suggestive: "Ireland's underdeveloped industrial sector was well known, and the absence of genuine workers in *Ulysses* cause for complaint by primitive Marxists. But the centrality of the press in the organization of Irish capitalism in the revolutionary period is at once a sign of industry's undeveloped state and its advanced consciousness, for control of communications takes the place of the steel-mills or the manufactories."[2]

The advanced state of the Irish press should be seen alongside other developments in the economic infrastructure, such as that of the railroads. The Irish rail system was one of the first in Europe. By 1914, it was one of the densest in the world, allowing the rapid dissemination throughout the country of modern English culture, and a doubling of the number of Irish newspapers and periodicals between 1853 and 1913.[3] With a very high rate of literacy, an urban population which included nearly as high a proportion of the professional middle classes as did England, and an educational establishment which, in 1878, had installed the "results system" ("introducing impersonal, rational, specialised criteria into the assessment of academic merit") and which had instituted the first chair of civil engineering in the United Kingdom (in 1844), Ireland was indeed in a position to explore at least some aspects of the advanced consciousness of modernity.[4]

Before turning to *Ulysses* and its social context, however, it is essential to examine once again the critical discourse which has taught us to read the book, as well as its culture. If there is a single origin for the critical paradigm of "spatial form" in modernist art, it is T. S. Eliot's brief essay, " 'Ulysses,' Order, and Myth," published in *The Dial* in 1922. Eliot argues that *Ulysses* is "the most important expression which the present age has found," that its "undisciplined" style is in fact precisely that new language necessary to permit the age to express itself, given the exhaustion of the traditional form of the novel. Though Eliot's delineation of the "mythical method" in this essay is familiar enough, some of its premises should be scrutinized again. For example, the essay's basic metaphor enables Eliot to draw far-reaching conclusions about the uses of history: "In using the myth, in manipulating a continuous parallel between contemporaneity and antiquity, Mr. Joyce is pursuing a method which others must pursue after him."[5]

Always conscious of the pastness of the past, Eliot figures the relation between antiquity and the present age to be like that of parallel lines, incapable of meeting, forever separated by an unbridgeable gap. And yet that parallel is "continuous." Somehow, reassuringly, the past is recoverable in all its wholeness. Even though it is never truly present to our own time, it is also not so broken or incomprehensible as to be inaccessible. It is our age which is fragmented and chaotic, of course, and the space which separates Eliot's parallel times turns out to be less an unbridgeable gap than a rhetorical hinge on which his arguments about reordering the present might turn.

The social usefulness of the mythical method for Eliot is quite explicit: "It is simply a way of controlling, or ordering, of giving a shape and a significance to the immense panorama of futility and anarchy which is contemporary history." Citing contemporary developments in psychology and ethnology, and in particular *The Golden Bough*, Eliot regards the manipulation of mythic parallels as an important new technique of control, a way of mastering a present which seems to have no center. By stepping outside of history, so to speak, we might hope to escape the chaos of modernity (though for Eliot himself, the hope seemed a forlorn one). That potential escape, however, takes place only in the terms of an idealist conception of art: the "panorama" of contemporary history is given "order" and "significance." The goal of the new experiments in artistic form, of which Joyce's novel seems to be exemplary, is simply to find a way of "making the modern world possible for art." For Eliot, this endeavor is a very private one: "And only those who have won their own discipline in secret and without aid, in a world which offers very little assistance to that end, can be of any use in furthering this advance." For writer and reader alike, the modernist project as Eliot sees it can only be a movement of the imagination, employing new techniques of artistic discontinuity to evade the "futility" of history. If the past is gone and the present a hopeless anarchy, at least in the empty space which divides them a kind of virtual order, a nostalgic continuity of the imagination, may be rebuilt.

Hugh Kenner has argued that Eliot's use of "myth" was "simply wrong."[6] He contends that Eliot's reading of *Ulysses* was highly selective, that the poet's famous essay was not likely to be challenged by readers who could not in fact read the banned novel. To Kenner, "myth" obscures the fact that contemporary archaeology had rescued Homer from Victorian romanticism and returned him to a historical reality which was very impressive to Joyce's generation. Although filled with mythological references, *Ulysses*, unlike the writings of most of the other great modernists, never attempts to transport the reader to "vanished times" or "mythological space." Its time is always 1904, and Kenner believes that its message is clear: "All is words, we are being reminded, and all words are now." In this reading, the formal discontinuities of Joyce's text do not lead us to a transcendent space where we can shelter from the chaos of modernity. On the contrary, these textual features permit Joyce to refuse "the most pervasive idea of the century in which he was born, the idea of continuity."[7] Against all notions of organic coherence, Joyce offers words, in the present.

In rejecting Eliot's mythic reading of *Ulysses*, Kenner offers "language" as a more elegant critical category: the novel's "stylistic variousness" would seem to be most striking to anyone actually paging through the book. By contending that the text's principal innovations lie in its play of many sublanguages, rather than in a manipulation of mythic parallels, Kenner suggests that Eliot's Joyce should be replaced by an author less concerned with transcendent pattern than with the materiality of language as it acts to shape history and human character. And his remarks on truth support this line of thought: "Still we may suppose that there is after all a 'truth' recoverable from beneath all these surfaces, a truth the writer could put straightforwardly if he wanted to. There is not."[8]

Kenner locates Joycean skepticism within an Irish context which he describes as "nearly perfect Pyrrhonism: a whole community agreed upon this one thing, that no one at bottom knows what he is talking about because there is nothing to know except the talk." It is at this point, however, where words are not a way out of history but quite simply an end in themselves, that Eliot, paradoxically, seems to return. In describing the Pyrrhonism of the Irish, Kenner emphasizes its aestheticism. He defines the dogma of skepticism as "that when statements can have no substance they can only have style. The style, moreover, is the man." It follows, then, that the battles of *Ulysses* would take place as "savage stylistic dissection," that the assessment of "surface and style" would constitute the entire world of the novel.[9] Even the many critics who have struggled to equip "the great affirmation of meaninglessness with meaning" have participated in this play of surfaces. The result for Kenner is very much like that cognitive game-playing (discussed earlier, in relation to Pound's writings) which, in *The Counterfeiters*, he ascribed to modernity's empiricism. Kenner's evaluation of the literary technique of juxtaposing multiple discourses is very different indeed from my own account of the social significance of similar textual strategies in Pound, Lawrence, and Williams.

For Kenner as for Eliot, however, the endless play of stylistic surfaces is not an occasion for Nietszchean joy, nor is it the starting point for an inquiry into the ways in which discourse structures the human subject. The play of language in the novel has its origin (according to Kenner) in an author/God who looms very large. Joyce finds himself incarnated in an Irish world from which he differs; its

Pyrrhonism forces him to present his authorship as mystery, issuing from a void, an absence. Kenner's continuing theme is the brilliance of Joyce as author, and even as he reminds us that style is the man, he assumes that there is a stable human reality beneath the contortions of language. Discussing the subtle resonances of diction, he notes that "it is with such tiny nudges that we are taught the right reading of the signatures of all things." If no single truth is recoverable from the multiple surfaces of Joyce's book, there is a shadowy "whole truth" which cannot be communicated, but which nevertheless does exist. "The True Sentence, in Joyce's opinion, had best settle for being true to the voice that utters it, and moreover had best acknowledge that when voices commence listening to themselves they turn into styles. . . . Style is a necessary evil."[10] Words may indeed be all there is in a book such as *Ulysses*, but that fragmentation is either a tragedy or a joke, and when Joyce's novel is regarded in this light, it becomes the nostalgic search for a voice capable of once more stabilizing the shifting surfaces of the human subject. For Kenner, that search involves an attack on objectivity, now understood to be an ephemeral movement within the larger realm of literature. While seeming to reject Eliot's mythical method, he in fact evades history just as effectively through an emphasis on stylistic variation as the reestablishment of the rhetorical play of author and muse. Irish skepticism is recontained by a metaphysical category: Rhetoric becomes the timeless human norm which trivializes all historical specificity.

Poststructuralist approaches to *Ulysses* have also taken the instability of Joyce's language as their starting point. The most ambitious attempt to consider Joyce along poststructuralist lines has been that of Colin MacCabe. Like many earlier critics, MacCabe is concerned with the stylistic diversity of *Ulysses*. In his case, however, this diversity is not to be explained in terms of an organic congruence (like that posited by Eliot) between literary form and the chaotic age it would express. Rather, the textual discontinuity of Joyce's work is understood by placing it beside the realist novel, where stylistic diversity is always contained by the presence in the text of a dominant style, or meta-language. In realism, that meta-language acts to suppress difference, and therefore desire, leading to a "neurotic" linguistic structure which prevents the reader from producing meaning through play in the materiality of language. For MacCabe, realist fiction, and the expectations which it demands of readers, are not the result of some natural evolution, but of institutional practices, including those of literary criticism. To examine the writing of Joyce in this light is thus to engage in a reflexive process in which neither text nor reader can be the stable origin of interpretation.

When a book such as *Ulysses* is contrasted with the novels of realism, it appears to refuse any meta-language: none of the various discourses within the novel is able to control or make sense of the others. Thus, according to MacCabe, Joyce's text is unlike the realist novel in that it is uncentered by the familiar narrative voice which subordinates all others to its own transparent truth. *Ulysses,* on the contrary, displays many voices, and so invites the reader to investigate the very process of signification. The importance of this function of the text is not so much to illuminate the nature of discourse, as it is to allow the reader to become aware of how he/she is situated within the text. In MacCabe's view, it is the constitution of the subject which is primarily at issue:

> I have suggested that the crucial difference for the reader of Joyce lies in the position allocated him or her by the text. Instead of a traditional organisation of discourses which confer an imaginary unity on the reader, there is a disruption of any such position of unity. The reader is transformed into a set of contradictory discourses, engaged in the investigation of his or her own symbolic construction. What is subverted in the writing is the full Cartesian subject and this subversion is a political event of central importance.[11]

Despite the political importance which he ascribes to the subversion of the notion of a unified subject, MacCabe argues that Joyce's writing is, in fact, politically ineffective.

The political failure of *Ulysses* rests, in MacCabe's view, on the fact that it does not have a definite notion of the audience to which it is addressed. Joyce seemed to assume the existence of a common reader for his writing, but that faith was mistaken. As a result, Joyce was himself the only audience inscribed in his texts, and thus an "immutable, individual human nature" was resurrected within a kind of writing designed to undermine precisely that identity. Rather than simply condemn Joyce's failure to address an audience, however, MacCabe attempts to explain it in historical terms. He argues that Joyce's support for Arthur Griffith and Sinn Fein began to wane when they capitulated to the repressive forces of the Church, which seemed to Joyce to be as destructive as the power of the British state. With the eventual triumph of the Free State, it seemed to Joyce that repression had simply assumed a new guise. All that remained possible was "a more and more desperate attempt to deconstruct those forms of identification which had allowed the triumph of the national revolution to mean the very opposite of a liberation of Ireland."[12]

Although he begins with the materiality of Joyce's text, with the interplay of discourses which effectively breaks the illusion that there is a "natural," unified subject, MacCabe seems to abandon that position by the end of his book. It is not entirely clear how a specific audience could be inscribed in the text without assuming a position like that of the meta-language which had always acted to deprive the reader of "the productive effects of his or her discourses." Nor, on the other hand, is it immediately evident why the openness of the text, and so the openness of one's own constitution as a subject, could only be learned through reading a text which already contained one's own prior identity inscribed as centering discourse. Moreover, while the Lacanian thrust of this argument is helpful in exploring the genealogy of cultural repression in Joyce's world, it remains on a very abstract level with regard to the analysis of discourse. If the textual openness of *Ulysses* encourages awareness of the social power of language, as I believe, it nevertheless remains necessary to delineate the specific discursive practices which characterize a given historical moment.[13]

II

In order to understand the extent to which Irish culture had become a part of modernity by the time Joyce wrote, it might be well to recall Georg Lukács's notion of reification, an elaboration of Marx's concept that under capitalism the relations among people take on the quality of relations among things, that the commodity structure of the market is reproduced in human intercourse, though that commodification of human relations is ordinarily invisible to those who experience it. Under this condition, "man's own activity, his own labour becomes something objective and independent of him, something that controls him by virtue of an autonomy alien to man." With regard to the subjective aspect of this situation, Lukács argues that "where the market economy has been fully developed—a man's activity becomes estranged from himself, it turns into a commodity which, subject to the non-human objectivity of the natural laws of society, must go its own way independently of man just like any consumer article."[14] Although Lukács, like Marx before him, was primarily concerned with the industrial world of the nineteenth-century factory, his line of argument was employed by others as a way of beginning to understand the gradually changing structures of advanced capitalism in the twentieth century.

The cultural consequences of technologically advanced systems of production were of particular concern to the members of the Frankfurt School. In his essay "The End of Reason," Max Horkheimer contemplated a world of work in which mechanization characterized the office as much as the factory, a world in which men who had formerly been "appendages to the machine" now became "appendages as such." Earlier techniques which had helped to accommodate men and women to the demands of industrial production (i.e., the instrumental reason which I have discussed in previous chapters) had been made unnecessary by a system responding to apparently irresistible, pervasive, "natural" laws. With the triumph of nominalism which enabled this system, reason could only regard objects "as a strange multiplicity, as a chaos."[15] Leveled by an economic reality which made all things equivalent through the mediation of money, "the proper being of the object is no longer taken into account." Such a world consists entirely of meaningless, uniform surfaces, and the men and women who live in it can only engage in the endless manipulation of objects—a category which now includes themselves.

The social criticism of the Frankfurt School rightly placed great emphasis on the media of mass communication in their analysis of the cultural impact of advanced industrialism. Popular arts, the press, and advertising appeared to play a crucial role in maintaining a system of production which depended on the widespread and uniform distribution of a discourse which foreclosed all questions except those of use. Language was the medium through which that distribution could be accomplished. Like so many other aspects of its world, however, language had assumed a kind of autonomy, a technological inevitability beyond the control of the individual. Here is Leopold Bloom, in the newspaper office, listening to the sound of the printing press: "Everything speaks in its own way. Sllt."[16] That Bloom should imagine that a machine could speak is somehow less surprising than his supposing that it speaks "in its own way." The many voices of "Aeolus" have long been described by critics, who more often than not ascribe them to the long-winded press—an institution which in its turn is regarded as a function of the Irish weakness for blather or, at best, high rhetoric. Whether their source is said to be in individuals or in the collective subject of "the Irish," however, the multiple languages of "Aeolus" are in no way the expression of any authentic subjectivity. Nothing (and no one) speaks in its own way in this chapter. When Bloom calls the machine "almost human," his anthropomorphizing comment might as easily be inverted: Bloom is moving through a society in which men and women speak, machine-like, the discourse which has constituted them.

Although the languages which are the matter of this chapter have received considerable attention from the critics, their deployment has seemed to be less interesting. Most striking, of course, is the typographical convention which would reduce every utterance to a headline or a caption. From pompous cliché to slightly obscene shorthand, the catalog of available styles, each one brief and boldface, seems to suggest that any meaning is transparent to the appropriate formula. Against this leveling uniformity, however, there runs an undercurrent of opposition, though often confused and anxious. Several pages before he listens to the printing press speak, Bloom is already thinking of machines: "Thumping thump. This morning the remains of the late

Mr. Patrick Dignam. Machines. Smash a man to atoms if they got him caught. Rule the world today" (118). Before he succeeds in "Humanizing" it, by imagining that it is gently trying to get his attention, Bloom thinks of the machine not only as dominating his world, but as threatening to tear a man apart. Though this potential fragmentation seems to contradict the enforced uniformities of public discourse, it does remain a persistent anxiety throughout the chapter. Here is Bloom a few pages later: "Funny the way those newspaper men veer about when they get wind of a new opening. Weathercocks. Hot and cold in the same breath. Wouldn't know which to believe. One story good till you hear the next. Go for one another baldheaded in the papers and then all blows over. Hailfellow well met the next moment" (125). If the men and women of this public world are as clear and stable as the headlines which presume to sum up their lives, they are at the same time as insubstantial as if they had been smashed to atoms.

Throughout the novel there is the sense that human identities are fragile, threatened. In Stephen's case, that is reason for hope as well as fear, and it takes a highly intellectualized form: "But I, entelechy, form of forms, am I by memory because under everchanging forms" (189). Stephen's self-understanding is abstract, invariably employing metaphysical or scientific terms: "Wait. Five months. Molecules all change. I am other I now. Other I got pound." Getting pounds, or not getting them, has a great deal to do with Stephen's present form, whether or not he prefers to think in more idealist terms. For Bloom, that economic reality is never far from his consciousness. To become another I is always a possibility for him, though not as the result of molecular entelechy, but as the ever-present threat of social disintegration in an economy characterized by continual change. Riding to Dignam's funeral he is reminded by an old man selling shoelaces of the terrible transformations that can take place in his world: old Tweedy had been a crown solicitor and now has only a silk hat, a mute thing, as emblem of his former state. Many pages later, in "Ithaca," Bloom's fear of a similar fate is expressed in an imaginative exercise which reduces him to "a negligible negative irrational unreal quantity" (725). What is particularly interesting about this passage is that it proceeds through a series of discrete steps consisting of general categories (e.g., poverty, mendicancy, destitution) and quite specifically defined social roles (e.g., the poor rate and deputy cess collector, fraudulent bankrupt, distributor of throwaways, etc.). Like the series of ready-made discursive patterns in "Aeolus," these tags fix men and women in a way which is as absolute as it is superficial. The power and clarity of a scheme of social identity such as this is inextricably involved with its contrary: an abyss of social disintegration, where identity is fragmented, smashed to atoms.[17]

When Bloom contemplates destitution or denounces machines as "supplanters, bugbears, manufactured monsters for mutual murder" (479), he seems to recall an earlier, romantic criticism of industrialization. But Bloom is really a man of the new century. His schemes sometimes may be utopian, but as often as not they represent a kind of entrepreneurship based on social planning rather than primary manufacture: "Of course if they ran a tramline along the North Circular from the cattle market to the quays value would go up like a shot" (58). A kind of Robert Moses in his fantasies, Bloom is interested in manipulating the relation between physical and cultural structures as a way of generating both wealth and social improvement. He speculates about the great potential of the nascent tourist industry, and when he does consider manufacturing, he is less like an Andrew Carnegie than like a Marin County visionary, imagining how he might recycle paper and extract the chemicals from human waste. By 1920 it was as clear to Joyce as to anyone that a man looking to succeed in the new hierarchy of work should aspire to the role of planner.

Dreams aside, the work Bloom actually performs in *Ulysses* is central to the emerging order in which economic function and personal identity are alike governed by language. Advertising exemplifies the ultimate nominalism of modernity, as it functions to equate people and things by means of a language rendered perfectly regular and instrumental. Before he goes to sleep each night, Bloom thinks about the perfect advertisement. Its main feature would be its efficiency, "all extraneous accretions excluded." As a special, rationalized language, such a mode of communication would eliminate everything not "congruous with the velocity of modern life" (720). Although he imagines this ideal conjunction between word and social formation, Bloom is well aware of more limited ways of exploiting the intertextuality of experience. Plumtree's Potted Meat, advertised amid the obituary notices, is his recurrent bad example, but his suggested design for the House of Keyes would use the subliminal power of the word to more positive effect: "The idea, Mr. Bloom said, is the house of keys. You know, councillor, the Manx parliament. Innuendo of home rule. Tourists, you know, from the isle of Man" (120). In a single image of crossed keys, the attention of Manx tourists is caught by familiarity, while for the Irish, political struggle is equated with selling tea. Like some universal solvent, the language of advertising reduces every object, interest, and group to an equivalence which enables their easy manipulation.

The reified state of social relations in the Dublin of *Ulysses* is most clear in "Nausicaa." Gerty MacDowell may be another of Joyce's tours de force in capturing the language of one of society's subgroups. But she is also a portrait of the subject constituted wholly by a discourse of things. If Gerty has received her identity from a tradition of popular romance, that genre of noble heroines and dark, mysterious strangers is itself in the service of a larger cultural discourse. This is the way just one small part of her self-identity is defined: "Why have women such eyes of witchery? Gerty's were of the bluest Irish blue, set off by lustrous lashes and dark expressive brows. Time was when those brows were not so silkilyseductive. It was Madame Vera Verity, directress of the Woman Beautiful page of the Princess novelette, who had first advised her to try eyebrowleine which gave that haunting expression to the eyes, so becoming in leaders of fashion, and she had never regretted it" (349). Gerty's eyes are described in language which already implies a familiar catalog of romance plots: "eyes of witchery," "dark expressive brows," "haunting expression." But just as the Princess novelette is an institution that unites literature and merchandising, so this series of images is merely one stage in a set of mutually transformable categories: selling cosmetics/personal identity/ literary meaning. Always suggesting a depth (of character, for example) which is never present, Truth in the figure of Vera Verity has become the perfect example of modernity's nominalism. An arbitrary name defines the subjectivity of countless young women, through the medium of fiction, by showing them how to "trade" on their looks.

Advertising is the modern art that most fully exemplifies this interweaving of private identity and public discourse. Like Bloom's crossed keys, the images created by advertising have no innate meanings, but only exist to facilitate the exchange of commodities among people who may as easily be defined as Irish patriots, or as mysteriously haunted lovers. All human relationships in this world take place in a kind of virtual space, where identities constituted by a general, instrumental rhetoric meet to carry out transactions of one kind or another. When Bloom and Gerty become lovers, their relationship is precisely of this sort. Each exists for the other only as a virtual image, Gerty for Bloom as "a hot little devil," Bloom for Gerty as "a foreigner the image of the photo she had of Martin Harvey, the matinee idol." Their interlude on the beach is not an aberration indulged in by two people who do not quite fit into their society, but rather an expression of their society's fundamental way of structuring human relationship.

From the spectacle of Miss Douce's smacked garter to the literal commodification of sex at the brothel, *Ulysses* is filled with men and women who have become objects for each other's gaze or use. But this condition is not confined to sexual relationship. Whether it be Father Conmee's concern to polish his social image (with arecanut toothpaste) or the Citizen's pamphlet patriotism, the people of Dublin speak lines already written for them. And here we might recall Frederick Taylor's prescription for managerial success once again: finding the right human raw material is no longer necessary; today we must make the new worker ourselves.[18] Such remaking is less like searching for iron ore than it is like writing a text. Bloom works on the fringes of this new enterprise.

III

One of the most striking features of *Ulysses* is the reflexiveness with which its characters are constructed for the reader. The continual juxtaposition of variant discourses assures that no single one can come to seem "natural," nor can subjectivity be regarded as existing apart from the socially created languages in which we must necessarily encounter it. Even in conservative, provincial Dublin, modernity becomes manifest in human relationships which have taken on much of the character of commodity exchange. Advertising would seem to be an appropriate figure for this nominalist world of political windbags and oily seducers.

The social significance of this absence of stable identity in Joyce's characters might be understood in terms of a further contention of the Frankfurt School. In their *Dialectic of Enlightenment*, Max Horkheimer and Theodor Adorno assert that the cultural crisis of the first half of the twentieth century is rooted in the Enlightenment tradition itself. In their view, "bourgeois society is ruled by equivalence. It makes the dissimilar comparable by reducing it to abstract quantities. To the Enlightenment, that which does not reduce to numbers, and ultimately to the one, becomes illusion; modern positivism writes it off as literature."[19] I have already discussed the danger that literature might support this condition by writing itself off—as did the work of Lawrence and, at times, Williams.

The modern principle of equivalence, for Horkheimer and Adorno, "excises the incommensurable," and it tolerates no Otherness: "Enlightenment is mythic fear turned radical. The pure immanence of positivism, its ultimate product, is no more than a so to speak universal taboo. Nothing at all may remain outside, because the mere idea of outsideness is the very source of fear." The effect of this rigorous exclusion reaches far beyond the structures of formal logic and science: "Not only are qualities dissolved in thought, but men are brought to actual conformity. The blessing that the market does not enquire after one's birth is paid for by the barterer, in that he models the potentialities that are his by birth on the production of the commodities that can be bought in the market."[20] The structure of knowledge is, in this view, inseparably involved with the constitution of the subject, and both are functions of their society's historically grounded system of exchange.

As a part of the Frankfurt School's critique of instrumental reason, this argument places great emphasis on the relation between knowledge as historically constituted, and power. For Horkheimer and Adorno, knowledge begins in a disenchantment of nature the purpose of which is to gain dominance over that nature and over other men. This knowledge as domination had its beginning when myth conquered a still more primitive animism, but it continues down to the present world of factory and bureaucrat, and its essence is technology. Governed by the Enlightenment's principle of equivalence through exclusion, knowledge which exists for purposes of mastery can have no place for pleasure or mystery.[21]

When the discourse of modernity is recast in these terms, the world of *Ulysses* seems at once familiar and discordant. The novel certainly calls our attention to the language of instrumental reason, whether in the "Oxen of the Sun" parody of nineteenth-century positivism—"Science, it cannot be too often repeated, deals with tangible phenomena. The man of science like the man in the street has to face hardheaded facts that cannot be blinked and explain them as best he can" (418)—or in Bloom's naive attempt to put great literature to practical use: "Concluding by inspection but erroneously that his silent companion was engaged in mental composition he reflected on the pleasures derived from literature of instruction rather than of amusement as he himself had applied to the works of William Shakespeare more than once for the solution of difficult problems in imaginary or real life" (677). From Mr. Deasy to the convivial schemers who people the streets of Dublin, reason is a tool, a way to solve practical problems.

For all his entrepreneurial plans and pathetic attempts at scientific self-improvement, though, Bloom's thoughts often deny the instrumentality of the age. When planning tram lines or labor-saving inventions, he seems a man of his times, but he can also be strangely archaic. There is an ambiguity about the modernity of Bloom's consciousness which might serve to critique the darker aspects of Horkheimer and Adorno's myth of the beginnings of civilization. In *Dialectic of Enlightenment*, they argue that the formation of the "civilized" self follows from Odysseus' most typical tactic of survival: the fundamental renunciation of his own identity. This gesture of renunciation is said to enable our very notion of the human:

> In class history, the enmity of the self to sacrifice implied a sacrifice of the self, inasmuch as it was paid for by a denial of nature in man for the sake of domination over non-human nature and over other men. This very denial, the nucleus of all civilizing rationality, is the germ cell of a proliferating mythic irrationality: with the denial of nature in

man not merely the *telos* of the outward control of nature but the *telos* of man's own life is distorted and befogged. As soon as man discards his awareness that he himself is nature, all the aims for which he keeps himself alive—social progress, the intensification of all his material and spiritual powers, even consciousness itself—are nullified, and the enthronement of the means as an end, which under late capitalism is tantamount to open insanity, is already perceptible in the prehistory of subjectivity.[22]

Defining Odysseus as "the self who always restrains himself," Horkheimer and Adorno ascribe the power of domination to this initial Western renunciation. By defining subjectivity as something apart from the natural world, which may henceforth be regarded as a lifeless object to be manipulated, civilized man embraced a weakness and isolation which the exemplary Odysseus had shown to be the paradoxical way to mastery. As Adorno's later work makes clear, the implications of this argument are not hopeful. At the very heart of rationality, there lies a renunciation which condemns the enlightened subject, now imprisoned in the rigid boundaries of his solitude, to wage perpetual war against the very nature of which he was once a part.

To many readers, Joyce's retelling of the myth of Odysseus has offered little more promise of cultural renewal than this dark German version, written in the shadow of fascism. But when the two are read together, the Irish fiction seems to draw an Odysseus who is not so inexorably caught by the history that defines him. To be sure, Bloom acts out the renunciations of civilization most painfully. In keeping with the transitory, nominalist categories which characterize advertising (the sphere in which he must survive), Bloom's identity seems almost as fragile as his name. This Henry Flower, Esq. is in some sense a Nobody who sacrifices his self in order to live by his wits. He is a practical man who would suppress spontaneous feeling, as did Odysseus, who beat on his breast in order to chastise his impetuous heart. But while such renunciatory enlightenment led only to self-destruction in the eyes of Horkheimer and Adorno, they had begun their study with the assumption "that social freedom is inseparable from enlightened thought" (xiii). Even though reason had come to justify new kinds of oppression, Odysseus' initial escape from myth into rationality still held out the promise of liberation.

And for Bloom, rationality, in the form of an inveterate intellectual curiosity, does constantly promise to undermine his bondage to the reified society of modern Dublin, a realm supposedly cut off from the natural world. In their discussion of the *Odyssey* as a crucial text in the formation of the civilized self, Horkheimer and Adorno note a transitional moment in that emergence which is peculiarly helpful in illuminating the contradictions of Bloom's behavior. While Odysseus has learned to master a newly objectified Nature, thereby founding his own subjectivity as something entirely independent of the world it would rule, Polyphemus has not yet crossed the margin that divides the primitive from the civilized. As a result, he has no stable self: "The giant's behavior has not yet become objectified in the form of 'character.' "[23] In this account, the absence of any notion of the individual subject, which is the weakness that allows Odysseus to defeat him, is at the same time Polyphemus' redeeming feature. He has not bought individual identity at the price of alienation from the natural world of which he is a part: "When he puts the young of his ewes and goats to their udders, the practical action includes concern for the creatures themselves; and, when he is blind, his famous speech to the leading ram whom he calls his friend and asks why this time he is the last of the flock to leave the cave, and whether he is saddened by his master's distress, is moving to a degree equalled only at the highest point of the Odyssey, when the returning wanderer is recognized by the old dog Argos." Though they are on opposite sides of the line which marks the beginning of civilization, Odysseus and Polyphemus are not yet so very far apart.

And scandalous as it might be to the notion of consistent narrative parallels, Bloom/Odysseus is also closer to his primitive adversary than we might imagine. The giant remains in a primitive state because he has not yet renounced his bond to nature, and so Bloom, like Polyphemus, often seems to forget his own separateness in sympathetic communication with a variety of animals: "Ay. Humane methods. Because the poor animals suffer and experts say and the best known remedy that doesn't cause pain to the animal and on the sore spot administer gently. Gob, he'd have a soft hand under a hen" (315). Bloom is the traveler who invariably brings home the dog with a sore paw, and who pities the street sweeper's horse ("But such a good poor brute, he was sorry he hadn't a lump of sugar"). He is even said (with great derision) to be capable of interest in the paltriest traces of the living world: "I declare to my antimacassar if you took up a straw from the bloody floor and if you said to Bloom: *Look at, Bloom. Do you see that straw? That's a straw.* Declare to my aunt he'd talk about it for an hour so he would and talk steady" (316). And, of course, this is the man subjected to public ridicule (by himself as well) because he doesn't really appear to be a man at all.

In the "Circe" episode, Bloom actually becomes a part of the animal world, at least in dream. And when he is transformed into a pig sniffing for truffles, his experience bears out Raymond Williams's reminder that Nature is always a concept shaped by history. Joyce complicates Homer in this sequence by drawing on the medieval equation of Nature with woman, the animal side of "Man," and so makes Bloom become not only an animal but a woman as well. If the equation is a medieval one, it still holds for modern aesthete and barroom sponge alike. Whether commenting on Miss Douce's garter-smacking performance in the pub ("Trained by owner") or on Molly's breasts ("But, by God, I was lost, so to speak, in the milky way"), the common wisdom of Dublin is that women are closer to the animal—or even mineral—world than they are to the "human." Nevertheless, throughout the novel, Bloom displays a desire to cross the space that divides the experience of men from women/nature. Amid the coarse jokes of the students at the lying-in hospital, he alone feels Mrs. Purefoy's ordeal. Milly's adolescence, and what it must mean to Molly, often occupies his imagination, while the lives of those women he meets more casually in the course of his travels invariably provoke at least a momentary identification.

When Bloom "sinks on all fours, grunting, snuffling, rooting" at the feet of Bella (now herself transformed into a man), he fully realizes his sympathetic identification with the animals and with his culture's equation of woman and Nature. But further, his incorporation into the natural world serves to make clear that the historically defined condition of Nature is one of submission to the domination of civilization: "Henceforth you are unmanned and mine in earnest, a thing under the yoke" (535). Bello makes a speech which explicitly defines his good bourgeois individuality in terms of its difference from the animal world he masters:

> I'll make you remember me for the balance of your natural life. (*His forehead veins swollen, his face congested.*) I shall sit on your ottoman-saddleback every morning after my thumping good breakfast of Matterson's fat ham rashers and a bottle of Guinness's porter. (*He belches.*) And suck my thumping good Stock Exchange cigar while I read the *Licensed Victualler's Gazette.* Very possibly I shall have you slaughtered and skewered in my stables and enjoy a slice of you with crisp crackling from the baking tin basted and baked like sucking pig with rice and lemon or currant sauce. It will hurt you. (532f.)

It is precisely during his "natural" life that Bloom will remember Bello's lesson: that no original state of Nature, innocent and self-sufficient, can ever be recovered, once civilization has appropriated the natural world to its own use and so redefined it as a private stockyard.

If Bloom's imagination is capable of carrying him back across the line dividing the human and the animal, and so of revealing the most general basis for Western civilization's ethos of mastery, it also works to undermine the instrumental reason which is modernity's version of that ancient ethos. Though Bloom spends much of his time speculating about this and that, his intellectual curiosity often ceases to be the cunning of a survivor and becomes simply wonder. Whether or not a cat needs its feelers to mouse is the sort of thing that scientists investigate, and the East might well repay study for one who is interested in the tourist business. But Bloom wants to know more than need would ever demand: "The far east. Lovely spot it must be: the garden of the world, big lazy leaves to float about on, cactuses, flowery meads, snaky lianas they call them. Wonder is it like that" (71). Beyond the knowledge he can hold and use, Bloom is interested in that which will always elude his understanding because it is too large, too distant, too incompatible with the forms of his knowing. Like my grandfather, who worked in the iron foundries of Chicago but thought about the shores of "the great Atlantic Ocean," Bloom is something of an anomaly.

Nowhere is Bloom's sense of wonder defined more clearly than in his interest in astronomy: "He's dead nuts on sales, McCoy said. I was with him one day and he bought a book from an old one in Liffey street for two bob. There were fine plates in it worth double the money, the stars and the moon and comets with long tails. Astronomy it was about" (233). Lenehan continues this exchange about Bloom's idiosyncrasies by recalling the time he had ridden home from a party with the Blooms. To Lenehan, Molly's "milky way" was all there was of interest, and he ridicules Bloom for having babbled on about the stars and constellations. What emerges from a passage such as this is not so much the cruelty of Lenehan and McCoy's laughter, as its reason: Bloom's behavior is a joke because it is absurd. They might scorn his practical inventions, but they cannot even recognize his sense of wonder because their society allows no space for purposeless thought. Lenehan and McCoy may be the comical dregs of Enlightenment culture, but they have learned its fundamental premise.

Bloom studies the heavens as an amateur. He loves them, and his wonder has no practical issue. Surely too trivial a kind of knowledge to be subversive, and yet it leads him in surprising directions. At the end of his travels, when we finally see him contemplate the night sky, he thinks "of our system plunging towards the constellation of Hercules: of the parallax or parallactic drift of socalled fixed stars, in reality evermoving from immeasurably remote eons to infinitely remote futures in comparison with which the years, threescore and ten, of allotted human life formed a parenthesis of infinitesimal brevity" (698). After Stephen leaves, Bloom feels "the cold of interstellar space, thousands of degrees below freezing point or the absolute zero of Fahrenheit, Centigrade or Réaumur: the incipient intimations of proximate dawn." The conventions of realism would dispense with these feelings easily: he is tired, and somewhat disappointed that Stephen chose not to stay. But Ulysses is not a realist fiction, and Bloom's thoughts are in fact more interesting. At the very moment in which he experiences an imaginative connection to the cosmos so intense that he feels the cold of outer space, he arrives at the clearest perception of his own isolation. Bloom understands the loneliness of his individuality only when he sees himself most fully as a part of nature, and only when the language of science has lost all practical import.

There is no real paradox here, of course. What Bloom has been forced to confront is simply the condition of his own individuality, which is a construction of civilization depending on the strict separation of ego from the natural world it presumes to govern. Only when thought, perhaps playfully, breaks the social fiction of that separation does the price exacted by such civilization become apparent. If Bloom's sense of wonder (which is subversive, because useless) can occasionally confound the discourse of practical use which dominates his day, it cannot overturn it. Literature is, after all, only a small part of modernity. And even Bloom, in his aspiration to be a kind of Irish Thomas Edison, helps to reproduce the dominant instrumentality of his age, just as, with another part of himself, he would resist it.

But Bloom's ambiguity does not mean that the modernism of *Ulysses* is either an ironic rejection of modernity altogether or the affirmation of sheer materiality in a kind of trans-historical yes. The men and women who people Joyce's Dublin live in our world of industrial production, mass media, and planned change. They understand the language of instrumental reason, that discourse which enabled the marriage of science and industry in the nineteenth century and which gradually came to include all knowledge under its reigning paradigm of "use." If they often see that paradigm as the expression of British imperialism, and attempt to reject it by embracing an ideology of mythic Irish heroism instead, their gesture is only mystification. Bloom, less deceived (though not undeceived), is a nationalist who scrambles for his niche in the economic order which is steadily transforming his world. When he broods about an advertisement that would be perfect in its transparency to all segments of society, he is like the Ulysses/Nobody who discovers that civilization consists in the manipulation of arbitrary codes. But he is also like that earlier Ulysses in that the margin he has crossed is still visible. A social man precisely because he has learned to be an isolated individual, Bloom also remains a part of nature. The doubleness of Bloom as a literary construction is not an ambiguity to be resolved or enjoyed, but rather the sign of modernism's complex engagement with history.

NOTES

Introduction

1. Studs Terkel, *Working* (New York, 1972), 48.
2. E. P. Thompson, *The Making of the English Working Class* (New York: Vintage, 1966), 292.
3. *Work in America* (Cambridge, Mass.: MIT Press, 1973), 22.
4. Randolph Bourne, "In the Mind of the Worker," *Atlantic Monthly* 113 (March 1914): 375–82.
5. James B. Gilbert, *Work without Salvation: America's Intellectuals and Industrial Alienation, 1880–1910* (Baltimore: Johns Hopkins University Press, 1977), 31–43.
6. Frederick Winslow Taylor, *The Principles of Scientific Management* (1911: rpt. New York: Norton, 1967), 6.
7. Ibid., 7.
8. In *Scientific Management since Taylor: A Collection of Authoritative Papers*, ed. Edward Eyre Hunt (New York: McGraw-Hill, 1924), 205f.
9. *Principles of Scientific Management*, 26.
10. Ibid., 36, 38.
11. Quoted in David Montgomery, *The Fall of the House of Labor: The Workplace, the State, and American Labor Activism, 1865–1925* (Cambridge: Cambridge University Press, 1987), 220f.
12. *Scientific Management since Taylor*, viii.
13. In *Scientific Management: A Collection of the More Significant Articles Describing the Taylor System of Management*, ed. Clarence Bertrand Thompson (Cambridge: Harvard University Press, 1914), 848.
14. Ibid., 856.
15. *Work in America*, 38. See also Daniel T. Rogers, *The Work Ethic in Industrial America 1850–1920* (Chicago: University of Chicago Press, 1978), 27, 125.
16. Montgomery, 459.
17. Morris Llewellyn Cooke, *Academic and Industrial Efficiency, Bulletin of the Carnegie Foundation for the Advancement of Teaching* (New York, 1910), iv.
18. Ibid., 24, iv.
19. Residents of Hull House, *Hull-House Maps and Papers* (New York, 1895), 169.
20. Michel Foucault, *Discipline and Punish: The Birth of the Prison*, trans. Alan Sheridan (New York: Random, 1979), 220f.
21. Richard Edwards, *Contested Terrain: The Transformation of the Workplace in the Twentieth Century* (New York: Basic Books, 1979), 148.
22. Michel Foucault, "Two Lectures," in *Power/Knowledge: Selected Interviews and Other Writings 1972–1977*, ed. Colin Gordon (New York: Pantheon, 1980), 97.
23. *Power/Knowledge*, 117; and *Language, Counter-Memory, Practice*, ed. Donald F. Bouchard (Ithaca: Cornell University Press, 1977), 43f., 139–64.
24. Lewis Mumford, *Technics and Civilization* (New York: Harcourt Brace, 1934), 365.
25. Ibid., 4, 3.
26. David F. Noble, *Forces of Production: A Social History of Automation* (New York: Alfred A. Knopf, 1984), xiii. See also Carroll Pursell, "The American Ideal of a Democratic Technology," in *The Technological Imagination: Theories and Fictions*, ed.

Teresa De Lauretis, Andreas Huyssen, and Kathleen Woodward (Madison, Wis.: Coda Press, 1980), 11–25.

27. Noble, xv.

28. Georg Lukács, *History and Class Consciousness* (Cambridge, Mass.: MIT Press, 1971), 88, 89.

29. Lukács, "The Ideology of Modernism," in *Realism in Our Time*, trans. John and Neeke Mander (New York: Harper & Row, 1971), 25.

30. Antonio Gramsci, *Selections from the Prison Notebooks*, ed. Quinton Hoare and Geoffrey Nowell Smith (New York: International Publishers, 1971), 34f.

31. Ibid., 9.

32. Cecilia Tichi, *Shifting Gears: Technology, Literature, Culture in Modernist America* (Chapel Hill: University of North Carolina Press, 1987), 76.

33. Ibid., 26.

34. Lisa M. Steinman, *Made in America: Science, Technology, and American Modernist Poets* (New Haven: Yale University Press, 1987), 22.

35. Montgomery (n. 11), 229.

36. Tichi and Steinman have offered the best accounts of modernist attempts to claim a wordly usefulness for the arts.

Chapter 1

1. Ezra Pound, "The City," in *Selected Prose 1909–1965*, ed. William Cookson (New York: New Directions, 1973), 224.

2. Maurice Beebe, "*Ulysses* and the Age of Modernism," in *Ulysses: Fifty Years* Thomas Staley, ed., (Bloomington: Indiana University Press, 1974), 175.

3. Donald Davie, *Ezra Pound: The Last Rower* (New York: Viking, 1976), p. 18; and Michael Reck, *Ezra Pound: A Close-Up* (New York: McGraw-Hill, 1967), 16.

4. Ezra Pound, "Ford Madox (Hueffer) Ford; Obit," in *Selected Prose*, p. 462.

5. Ford Madox Ford, *Thus to Revisit* (1921; rpt. New York: Octagon, 1966), 69.

6. Ibid., 52.

7. Pound, *Selected Prose*, 318, 432, 462.

8. Edmund Wilson, *Axel's Castle* (New York: Scribner's, 1931), 266, 292, 298.

9. Raymond Williams, "Means of Communication as Means of Production," in *Problems in Materialism and Culture* (London: Verso Editions, 1980), 50; see also Walter Benjamin, "The Author as Producer," in *Reflections* (New York: Harcourt, 1978), 233.

10. Pound, "Hudson: Poet Strayed into Science," *Selected Prose*, 430.

11. Pound, *Selected Prose*, 431.

12. W. H. Hudson, *A Shepherd's Life*. vol. 23 in *The Collected Works of W. H. Hudson* (London: J. M. Dent, 1923), 103.

13. Ibid., 215.

14. Ibid., 291.

15. Ibid., 332.

16. Raymond Williams, *Culture and Society, 1780–1950* (New York: Columbia University Press, 1958), 140.

17. Hudson, *A Shepherd's Life*, 290.

18. Pound, *Selected Prose*, 432.

19. Ford Madox Ford, *England and the English* (New York: McClure, Phillips, 1907), 218f.

20. Richard A. Cassell, "Images of Collapse and Reconstruction: Ford's Vision of Society," *ELT* 19, no. 4 (1976): 279; Norman Leer, *The Limited Hero in the Novels of Ford Madox Ford* (East Lansing: Michigan State University Press, 1966), 17.

21. Pound, *Selected Prose*, 463.

22. Ford, *England and the English*, 64.

23. Ibid., 20. For an account of some of the implications of the German example, see Harry Braverman, *Labor and Monopoly Capital: The Degradation of Work in the Twentieth Century* (New York and London: Monthly Review Press, 1974), 141–44, 159–63.

24. Ford, *England and the English*, 30.

25. Ibid., 64.

26. "Patria Mia," in *Selected Prose*, 108.

27. George Santayana, *Character and Opinion in the United States* (New York: Scribner's, 1920), 14.

28. Ibid., 20, 22.

29. Ibid., 55–56.

30. Pound, *Selected Prose*, 195.

31. Ibid., 192.

32. Frederick Winslow Taylor, *The Principles of Scientific Management* (1911; rpt., New York: Norton, 1967), 7.

33. Tichi, *Shifting Gears*, 79.

34. Pound, "Patria Mia," in *Selected Prose*, 111.

35. Hunt, *Scientific Management since Taylor*, viii.

36. *Selected Prose*, 114.

37. Paul Smith, *Pound Revised* (London: Croom Helm, 1983), 29.

38. Ezra Pound, *Personae* (New York: New Directions, 1926), 194.

Chapter 2

1. *The Cantos of Ezra Pound* (New York: New Directions, 1970), 60.

2. Tristan Tzara, "Lecture on Dada" (1924), in Herschel B. Chipp, ed., *Theories of Modern Art: A Source Book by Artists and Critics* (Berkeley: University of California Press, 1968), 388.

3. Paul Fussell, *The Great War and Modern Memory* (New York: Oxford University Press, 1975); Marshall Berman, *All That Is Solid Melts into Air* (New York: Simon & Schuster, 1982).

4. T. S. Eliot, *Selected Essays* (New York: Harcourt, 1932), 248.

5. Joseph Frank, "Spatial Form in Modern Literature," in *The Widening Gyre: Crisis and Mastery in Modern Literature* (Bloomington: Indiana University Press, 1968), 56. For some sense of the continuing controversy over the notion of spatial form, see Frank's "Spatial Form: An Answer to Critics," *Critical Inquiry* 4 (1977): 231–52; and his "Spatial Form: Some Further Reflections," *Critical Inquiry* 5 (1978): 275–90; also see Reed Dasenbrock, *The Literary Vorticism of Ezra Pound and Wyndham Lewis* (Baltimore: Johns Hopkins University Press, 1985), 139ff.

6. Frank, "Spatial Form," 60.

7. In Thompson, ed. *Scientific Management*, 848f.

8. Philip Rahv, "The Myth and the Powerhouse," in *The Myth and the Powerhouse* (New York: Farrar, Strauss & Giroux, 1965), 6, 14, 20.

9. Cleanth Brooks, *Modern Poetry and the Tradition* (Chapel Hill: University of North Carolina Press, 1939), 171f.

10. Ibid., 43–46. See also Gerald Graff's critique of "theories which ascribe to poetry a self-validating, independent contextual principle," a premise which, he shows, is shared by new critics and mythopoeic critics alike; in *Poetic Statement and Critical Dogma* (Evanston, Ill.: Northwestern University Press, 1970), 68.

11. Allen Tate, "Four American Poets," in *Reactionary Essays on Poetry and Ideas* (New York: Scribner's, 1936), 49.

12. Hugh Kenner, *The Counterfeiters* (Bloomington: Indiana University Press, 1968), 40, 172.

13. Ibid., 173, 147.

14. Georg Lukács, "The Ideology of Modernism," in *Realism in Our Time* (New York: Harper & Row, 1964), 17.

15. Ibid., 21.

16. Frederic Jameson, *Marxism and Form* (Princeton: Princeton University Press, 1971), 200. For two related views see Alan Wilde, *Horizons of Assent* (Princeton: Princeton University Press, 1981), 10; and Ihab Hassan, *The Dismemberment of Orpheus* (New York: Oxford University Press, 1971), 21.

17. Lukács, *Realism in Our Time*, 36.

18. Joseph Riddel, "Decentering the Image: The 'Project' of 'American' Poetics," in *Textual Strategies: Perspectives in Post-Structuralist Criticism*, ed. Josué V. Harari (Ithaca, N.Y.: Cornell University Press, 1979), 322–58.

19. Ibid., 342.

20. Weldon Thornton, *J. M. Synge and the Western Mind* (New York: Barnes & Noble, 1979), 98.

21. Gerald Graff, *Literature against Itself: Literary Ideas in Modern Society* (Chicago: University of Chicago Press, 1979), 70.

22. Edward Said, *The World, The Text and the Critic* (Cambridge: Harvard University Press, 1983), 4.

23. Pound, *Selected Prose*, 195.

24. Ezra Pound, "Affirmations: Analysis of this Decade," in *Ezra Pound and the Visual Arts*, ed. Harriet Zinnes (New York: New Directions, 1980), 27f.

25. Ibid., 299–302.

26. Dasenbrock, *The Literary Vorticism of Ezra Pound and Wyndham Lewis*, 47, 46.

27. Quoted in *Ezra Pound and the Visual Arts*, 302f.

28. Edward Eyre Hunt, ed., *Scientific Management since Taylor: A Collection of Authoritative Papers* (New York: McGraw-Hill, 1924), xi.

29. Judith A. Merkle, *Management and Ideology: The Legacy of the International Scientific Management Movement* (Berkeley: University of California Press, 1980), 235.

30. Marcia Landy, *Fascism in Film: The Italian Commercial Cinema, 1931–1943* (Princeton: Princeton University Press, 1986), 175, 176.

31. Taylor, *The Principles of Scientific Management*, 10, 142f., 140f.

32. *The Cantos of Ezra Pound*, 187.

33. David F. Noble, *Forces of Production*, 70.

34. *Selected Prose*, 183.

35. Thompson, ed., *Scientific Management*, 735.

36. Ibid., 739.

37. Pound, *Selected Prose*, 444.

38. *The Cantos of Ezra Pound*, 63.

39. Dexter S. Kimball, *Industrial Economics* (New York: McGraw-Hill, 1929), 259.

40. Ibid., 79.

41. Paul Smith, *Pound Revised* (London: Croom Helm, 1983), 61.

42. *The Cantos of Ezra Pound*, 190.

43. Ernest Fenollosa, *The Chinese Written Character as a Medium for Poetry*, ed. Ezra Pound (1920; rpt., San Francisco: City Lights, n.d.), 28, 12.

44. Pound, *Selected Prose*, 25.

45. *The Cantos of Ezra Pound*, 99f.

46. Ibid., 235.

47. Ibid., 250.

Chapter 3

1. D. H. Lawrence, *Women in Love* (New York: Viking, 1960), viii.

2. D. H. Lawrence, *Studies in Classic American Literature* (New York: Viking, 1964), 2.

3. Frank Kermode, *D. H. Lawrence* (New York: Viking, 1973), 14.

4. Michael Ragussis, *The Subterfuge of Art: Language and the Romantic Tradition* (Baltimore: Johns Hopkins University Press, 1978), 176f.

5. Victor Turner, "Social Dramas and Stories about Them," in *On Narrative*, ed. W. J. T. Mitchell (Chicago: University of Chicago Press, 1981), 146, 153.

6. Christopher Caudwell, *Studies in a Dying Culture* (London: John Lane, 1938), 58ff.

7. *Women in Love*, 223.

8. Hubert Zapf, "Taylorism in D. H. Lawrence's *Women in Love*," *D. H. Lawrence Review* 15, nos. 1–2 (Spring–Summer 1982): 129–39, has pointed out parallels between Taylor's scientific management and *Women in Love*, though he takes Lawrence's narrative as a realistic and radical social critique, in contrast to my view that the discursive context of Lawrence's novel makes its social stance more complex and problematic.

9. E. P. Thompson, *The Making of the English Working Class* (New York: Vintage, 1966), 243.

10. Frederick Winslow Taylor, *The Principles of Scientific Management* (1911; rpt., New York: Norton, 1967), 36–38, 53ff. For a discussion of the origins of scientific management in British industry, including practices which, as early as 1890, had anticipated Taylor's theories, see E. J. Hobsbawm, *Labouring Men: Studies in the History of Labour* (London: Weidenfeld & Nicolson, 1964), 355–62. Also, Sidney Pollard, *The Genesis of Modern Management: A Study of the Industrial Revolution in Great Britain* (Cambridge: Harvard University Press, 1965), 250–59.

11. Taylor, 38; David F. Noble, *America by Design* (Oxford: Oxford University Press, 1977), 3–49; Harry Braverman, *Labor and Monopoly Capital* (New York: Monthly Review Press, 1974), 124–37.

12. Lawrence, *Women in Love*, 215.

13. Ibid., 223.

14. Ibid., 209, 221.

15. Lawrence, *Studies in Classic American Literature*, 21.

16. D. H. Lawrence, "Study of Thomas Hardy," in *Phoenix*, ed. Edward D. McDonald (New York: Viking, 1936), 424.

17. Lawrence, *Women in Love*, 324.

18. Lawrence, *Phoenix*, 424, 423, 220.

19. Ibid., 223.

20. Ibid., 178, 423.

21. Judith A. Merkle, *Management and Ideology: The Legacy of the International Scientific Management Movement* (Berkeley: University of California Press, 1980), 224.

22. Geoffrey H. Hartman has noted the modern tendency to restrict the "work" of understanding to "productive" activities, but he regards this vital change as the result of curiously ahistorical "attitudes." See *Criticism in the Wilderness* (New Haven: Yale University Press, 1980), 166.

23. Lawrence, *Women in Love*, 223.

24. Merkle, 224ff.

25. Lawrence, *Women in Love*, 223.

26. Aidan Burns, *Nature and Culture in D. H. Lawrence* (Totowa, N.J.: Barnes & Noble, 1980), 80.

27. David F. Noble, *Forces of Production: A Social History of Industrial Automation*, 248.

28. Lawrence, *Women in Love*, 223, 220.

29. Herbert A. Simon, *The Sciences of the Artificial* (Cambridge: MIT Press, 1969), 83.

30. Graff argues that "industrialism intensified the separation of fact and value by institutionalizing objective thought in the form of technology, commerce, and, later, bureaucracy, administration, and social engineering. 'Reason' thus became equated with amoral mechanism, with the commerical calculus of profit and the laissez-faire economy, with means and instrumental efficiency over ends, with a regimented,

overorganized society which destroys ritual, folk customs, and the heroic dimension of life." In *Literature Against Itself, 41.*

Chapter 4

1. David Lodge, "The Language of Modernist Fiction: Metaphor and Metonymy," in *Modernism*, ed. Malcolm Bradbury and James McFarlane (Harmondsworth: Penguin, 1976), 482; and Frank Kermode, "The Novels of D. H. Lawrence," in *D. H. Lawrence: Novelist, Poet, Prophet*, ed. Stephen Spender (New York: Harper & Row, 1973), 86.

2. Robert Langbaum, *The Mysteries of Identity: A Theme in Modern Literature* (New York: Oxford University Press, 1977), 301f.

3. Terry Eagleton, *Criticism and Ideology* (London: Verso, 1978), 160f.

4. Kermode, 84f.

5. D. H. Lawrence, *Women in Love* (New York: Viking, 1960), 305. Subsequent references in the text are also to pages in this edition of *Women in Love.*

6. M. M. Bakhtin, "Discourse in the Novel," in *The Dialogic Imagination*, ed. Michael Holquist (Austin: University of Texas Press, 1981), 271f.

7. *Ibid.*, 366f.

8. D. H. Lawrence, *The Rainbow* (New York: Viking, 1961), 2. Subsequent references in the text are also to pages in this edition of *The Rainbow.*

9. Daniel Albright, *Personality and Impersonality: Lawrence, Woolf, and Mann* (Chicago: University of Chicago Press., 1978), 50.

10. Stanley Aronowitz offers a critique of the major theoretical approaches to this issue in *False Promises: The Shaping of American Working Class Consciousness* (New York: McGraw-Hill, 1974), 51–133.

11. See Herbert Marcuse, *Eros and Civilization: A Philosophical Inquiry into Freud* (New York: Vintage, 1962), and *Counterrevolution and Revolt* (Boston: Beacon Press, 1972); and Gerald Graff's critique of Marcuse, in *Literature Against Itself, 68–77, 98–101.*

12. Scott Sanders, *D. H. Lawrence: The World of the Five Major Novels* (New York: Viking, 1974), 78.

13. Langbaum, 5.

14. Marguerite Beede Howe, *The Art of the Self in D. H Lawrence* (Athens: Ohio University Press, 1977) 1.

15. Frederic Jameson, *The Political Unconscious: Narrative as a Socially Significant Act* (Ithaca: Cornell University Press, 1981), 221.

Chapter 5

1. *Interviews with William Carlos Williams*, ed. Linda Welshimer Wagner (New York: New Directions, 1976), 19.

2. *The Collected Earlier Poems of William Carlos Williams* (New York: New Directions, 1966), 368; hereafter cited as CEP.

3. William Carlos Williams, *In the Money* (New York: New Directions, 1940), 179f. 182; hereafter IM.

4. William Carlos Williams, *White Mule* (New York: New Directions, 1937), 90ff.

5. William Carlos Williams, *The Doctor Stories*, ed. Robert Coles (New York: New Directions, 1984), 92–98.

6. William Carlos Williams, "The Descent of Winter," in *Imaginations*, ed. Webster Schott (New York: New Directions, 1970), 254; hereafter, I.

7. *A Recognizable Image: William Carlos Williams on Art and Artists*, ed. Bram Dijkstra (New York: New Directions, 1978), 97; hereafter RI.

8. *The Selected Letters of William Carlos Williams* (New York: New Directions, 1984), 18.

9. William Carlos Williams, *Selected Essays* (New York: New Directions, 1954), 11; hereafter SE.

10. William Carlos Williams, *The Embodiment of Knowledge*, ed. Ron Loewinsohn (New York: New Directions, 1974), 113; hereafter EK.

11. Lewis Mumford, *Technics and Civilization* (New York: Harcourt, Brace, 1934), 365.

12. For example, David F. Noble, *Forces of Production* (New York: Oxford University Press, 1986), ivf.

13. William Carlos Willams, *The Collected Later Poems* (New York: New Directions, 1963), 115; hereafter, CLP.

14. William Carlos Williams, *Autobiography* (New York: New Directions, 1967), 361; hereafter A.

15. William Carlos Williams, *In the American Grain* (New York: New Directions, 1925), hereafter IAG.

16. Stephen J. Greenblatt, *Renaissance Self-Fashioning: From More to Shakespeare* (Chicago: University of Chicago Press, 1980), 227.

17. D. H. Lawrence, *Studies in Classic American Literature*, 21.

18. Linda Welshimer Wagner, *The Prose of William Carlos Williams* (Middletown: Wesleyen University Press, 1970), 32, 8.

Chapter 6

1. William Carlos Williams, *Autobiography* (New York: New Directions, 1967), 333.

2. Ibid.

3. Leo Marx, *The Machine in the Garden: Technology and the Pastoral Ideal in America* (London and New York: Oxford University Press, 1964), 355f.

4. Ibid., 356.

5. Bram Dijkstra, ed., *A Recognizable Image: William Carlos Williams on Art and Artists* (New York: New Directions, 1978), 23, 22.

6. Ibid., 144, 147f.

7. Marjorie Perloff, *The Poetics of Indeterminacy: Rimbaud to Cage* (Princeton: Princeton University Press, 1981), 109–54, 151.

8. Joseph N. Riddel, "'Keep Your Pecker Up'—*Paterson Five* and the Question of Metapoetry," *Glyph* 8 (1981): 230, 207.

9. Joseph N. Riddel, *The Inverted Bell* (Baton Rouge: Louisiana State University Press, 1974), 114, 294.

10. Riddel, *Glyph*, 218.

11. William Carlos Williams, *Paterson* (New York: New Directions, 1963), 66f; hereafter P.

12. *New Jersey: A Guide to Its Present and Past*, compiled and written by the Federal Writers Project of the Works Progress Administration for the State of New Jersey (New York: Viking, 1939), 353, 80, 79.

13. Sue Ainslee Clark and Edith Wyatt, "Scientific Management as Applied to Women's Work," in Thompson, *Scientific Management*, 807–34.

14. John Dos Passos, *The Big Money* (New York: Harcourt, Brace, 1933), 21.

15. Benjamin Sankey, *A Companion to William Carlos Williams's Paterson* (Berkeley: University of California Press, 1971), 48.

16. William Carlos Williams, *The Embodiment of Knowledge*, ed. Ron Loewinsohn (New York: New Directions, 1974), 45.

17. Philip Rahv, "Religion and the Intellectuals," reprinted in *Essays on Literature and Politics, 1932–1972*, ed. Arabel J. Porter and Andrew J. Dvosin (Boston: Houghton Mifflin, 1978), 316.

18. Ibid., 309.

19. Philip Rahv, "Dostoevsky in *Crime and Punishment*," in *The Myth and the Powerhouse* (New York: Farrar, Strauss & Giroux, 1965), 115.

20. Ibid., 12.

21. Joel Conarroe, *William Carlos Williams' Paterson: Language and Landscape* (Philadelphia: University of Pennsylvania Press, 1970), 10.

22. Bram Dijkstra, *A Recognizable Image*, 15.

23. Raymond Williams, "Ideas of Nature," in *Problems in Materialism and Culture: Selected Essays* (London: Verso, 1980), 70.

24. Ibid., 78.

25. Ibid., 84.

26. *Interviews with William Carlos Williams*, ed. Linda Welshimer Wagner (New York: New Directions, 1976), 56.

Chapter 7

1. W. J. McCormack, *Ascendancy and Tradition in Anglo-Irish Literary History from 1789 to 1939* (Oxford: Clarendon Press, 1985), 217, 299.

2. Ibid., 288.

3. Joseph Lee, *The Modernisation of Irish Society, 1848–1918* (Dublin: Gill & Macmillan, 1973), 13.

4. Ibid.; 30, 18, 29–34. However, he qualifies the often expressed idea that Ireland was a "social laboratory" for England, 34ff.

5. T. S. Eliot, "'Ulysses,' Order, and Myth," in *Selected Prose of T. S. Eliot*, ed. Frank Kermode (New York: Harcourt, 1975), 177.

6. Hugh Kenner, *Joyce's Voices* (Berkeley: University of California Press, 1978), 64.

7. Ibid., 48, 49.

8. Ibid., 91.

9. Ibid., 53, 56.

10. Ibid., 27, 90.

11. Colin MacCabe, *James Joyce and the Revolution of the Word* (New York: Barnes & Noble, 1979), 152f.

12. Ibid., 170.

13. For another version of the argument that linguistic openness may be used to oppose historical constraint, see Seamus Deane, "Joyce and Nationalism," in *James Joyce: New Perspectives*, ed. Colin MacCabe (Bloomington: Indiana University Press, 1982), 168–183.

14. Georg Lukács, *History and Class Consciousness* (Cambridge: MIT Press, 1971), 87.

15. Max Horkheimer, "The End of Reason," in *The Essential Frankfurt School Reader*, ed. Andrew Arato and Eike Gebhardt (New York: Continuum, 1982), 38, 31.

16. James Joyce, *Ulysses* (New York: Random House, 1961), 121. All references are to this edition.

17. The human fragmentation which *Ulysses* depicts might be seen to support Terry Eagleton's contention that the poststructuralist desire to deconstruct the notion of the "unified subject" is largely misguided, since capitalist culture has already accomplished this process of fragmentation "much more efficiently than meditations on *écriture*"; in "Capitalism, Modernism, and Postmodernism," in *Against the Grain: Essays 1975–1985* (London: Verso, 1986), 145.

18. Frederick W. Taylor, *The Principles of Scientific Management* (1911; rpt., New York: Norton, 1967), 6.

19. Max Horkheimer and Theodor Adorno, *Dialectic of Enlightenment* (New York: Continuum, 1982), 7.

20. Ibid., 16, 12f.

21. Ibid., 5.

22. Ibid., 54.

23. Ibid., 66.

INDEX